PRAISE FOR
THE STORY CODE

The Story Code is more than just a book; it's like having a heart-to-heart with a wise friend who's been there. Mark has a way of making you see the stories you tell yourself and how they shape your world. He gives you the tools to rewrite those stories, embrace your strengths and dare to dream a brighter future. If you're feeling stuck or just need a little nudge, this book is your sign to take the leap – you won't regret it!

**– Nicola Nel, global managing director,
PROI Worldwide**

Mark Jones has cracked the code on something every executive faces but few address: the internal narratives that sabotage our success. *The Story Code* delivers what most leadership books miss – a clear, actionable framework for rewriting the stories that keep us stuck. As someone who's built brands and led teams, I can tell you this work on your internal narrative is the foundation everything else builds on. Essential reading for any leader serious about sustainable success.

– Deeps Ramanathan, global technology executive

Mark Jones's book *The Story Code* is kind, optimistic and energetic. He brings the reader along with warmth and humour, while not papering over some of the hardships of our work life. I particularly appreciated his honesty in including his own hard-won knowledge in these pages, and how it has cultivated many of the themes of his book.

– David Newman, narrative therapist,
Sydney Narrative Therapy

I've known Mark Jones for a long time and have always respected his thoughtful and respectful approach to understanding the impact of technology change and engaging with people. Sharing his experience and guidance in dealing with lack of self-belief and intense stress will help many people.

– Steve Vamos, author, speaker, advisor,
former CEO Xero and NineMSN, and
executive with IBM, Apple and Microsoft

This book puts the pen back in our hands. It reminds us that when life speeds up, the foundations of mental fitness and wellbeing can help us change the story we tell ourselves and each other. *The Story Code* is compassionate, evidence-aware and immediately useful.

– Belinda Elworthy, CEO Gotcha4Life Foundation

Mark Jones uses a scalpel to open up and go deep inside himself, pulling back the curtain on issues leaders are facing today, how we got here and what we can do about it. The framework we're taught presents us with steps that we need to take to pivot for more meaningful impact in life, or even to prevent a possible crash into his proverbial tree. Part memoir, part leadership and wellbeing treatise, this book serves up the case and means for reframing our beliefs in a way that's hard to deny and easy to implement.

– Natalie Mina, communication strategist and executive wayfinder

Story connects our past to present and sets platforms for our futures. Story connects our reality with intangible and mysterious worlds of imagination. In these pages, you will see Mark's story, people you know, and you will see your own. When you take the chance to deeply reflect on your story, your identity and belonging, you can feel more at home in yourself and with others. When you take the time to be intentional about your narrative, you can find your home within. I commend you to read this book, reflect on your story, and use the Story Code to find your way home.

– Mark Yettica-Paulson, Chief Super Native Unlimited

THE
STORY
CODE
FOR LEADERS

MARK JONES

JOURNALIST AND MINDSET STRATEGIST

THE STORY CODE

FOR LEADERS

Unlock resilience and influence
by rewriting the stories you tell yourself

First published in 2025 by Dean Publishing
PO Box 119
Mt. Macedon, Victoria, 3441
Australia
deanpublishing.com

DEAN PUBLISHING

Cataloguing-in-Publication Data
National Library of Australia

Title: The Story Code For Leaders
ISBN: 978-0-648995-75-3
Category: Self-help/success

To Heather, Emily, Daniel, Toby and Ethan –

for the love that leaves me wordless.

CONTENTS

PROLOGUE

SATURDAYS WILL NEVER BE THE SAME

I always loved Saturday. It brought a happy state of mind.

The oldest of four children growing up on the North Shore of Sydney in the 1980s, I was a busy young man. Responsible, and on the hustle. My first job was a paper run, which – for anyone under 30 – means you get paid a fixed amount to deliver a free local newspaper to houses within a ten-block radius of your house.

I also had other jobs like delivering prescription medicines on my bike from the chemist to elderly customers around the neighbourhood. Then there was my gig at the local fruit and vegetable shop, which was owned and run by a family of Italian immigrants. The men stocked shelves and drove fork-lifts while their wives worked the cash registers and shouted orders at anyone within earshot. My job was to carry boxes of fruit and veggies from the cash registers to customers' vehicles. A woman would scream, "Box out!" and I'd come scurrying, lift the box to my shoulder and walk with the customer to their car. It was pretty good work for a young bloke despite the intensity of being told what to do all the time.

And so, the weeks rolled on. A steady mix of school, casual work, homework, eating and sleeping.

Then came Saturdays.

Saturdays were hanging out with friends, riding my bike and doing chores around the house. This day felt like freedom from routine. It was the chance to get a bit creative.

Looking back, it's interesting just how simple and

uncomplicated life was in these pre-internet, pre-mobile phone days. I didn't know it then, but my weekly rhythm was setting up a pattern for life.

Subconsciously, I was writing a story in my head about how life was going to play out. Expectations creep up on you slowly like that.

Unlike some of my friends' home lives, mine was largely free of drama. I had a few tough moments in school with some teasing, and in early high school a couple of schoolyard fights. Mostly because I was pushed just that bit too far! One bloke thought it would be fun to throw the contents of my backpack across the room in music class – a grand sweeping gesture that spread everything, everywhere. Metres outside the classroom, I clocked him across the top of the head, and a tangle of limbs on the concrete followed. But honestly, that was about it.

Contrast that with the life of my younger brother, Glen, who had plenty of health issues in his early years. Middle ear infections, operations on his hearing and a dramatic reset of his jaw so he could eat properly. I quite enjoyed telling Mum I was 'economical'. No hospital or healthcare expenses for me, thanks very much!

And so began a positive, progressive climb in my young life. As the economists would understand, I started to picture my life on a chart that began in the bottom left corner of an X-Y axis and steadily climbed to the top right corner. Sure enough, as life progressed, things largely panned out as expected.

My wife Heather and I married young. At just 21 years old, and 6 months into our first grown-up jobs, we set about doing life together. We'd graduated from Western Sydney University together after meeting in first year. And wow, didn't we feel so grown-up! Adult friends thought we were 'babies', which in truth, we were.

Yet with our emerging careers in journalism and public relations, life was exciting, full of energy and fun times with friends and family. The world promised everything, and there was no reason to doubt it – aside from the usual anxieties and nervousness that come with learning about the world of work.

Then, amid it all, I had Saturdays. Work went on hold, and I got to fix stuff around the house, tinker with my car and catch up with friends.

As the years passed and children arrived, the routine of Saturdays remained. There was a rhythm to life and a shared understanding of how things work. Heather would later wisely observe that pottering around the house was good for my mental health.

On Saturdays, I got lost in the meditative hum of my lawnmower, satisfyingly taking rubbish to the tip and washing the car.

The trouble with expectations, however, is they tend to clash with reality at some point.

* * *

Skip forward to a fateful Saturday in late 2019.

Now 45 years old, I was a proper middle-aged married bloke with four kids, a big mortgage and was CEO of a brand story-telling agency Heather and I had co-founded a decade earlier. Filtered Media employed about 25 people and dominated most of my waking hours, plus a few of my midnight hours.

In fact, we'd hit some hard times in recent years. Client losses, messy internal processes and people dramas were less than fun. I was carrying the weight heavily (physically and mentally). I'd been soldiering on for months and years. Day in, day out. And like some kind of middle-aged textbook case, I was quickly going grey.

And so it rolled around, this fateful Saturday morning when I woke up with a strange headache. A faint one, to be fair. Not quite full-on, but definitely *there*. *But I have plans for the day*, I told myself. We had a big lawn that needed mowing, and I needed to buy gardening stuff from Bunnings.

In moments like this, my normal plan of attack was simple: have a coffee or two, down a Panadol, drink some Coca-Cola, and get on with it. Most of the time, caffeine saved the day for me, and I could carry on. The lawns would get done. I'd have my moment in the garden and enjoy the satisfaction of a job well done.

But on this day, standing in the kitchen at our home in Wahroonga and looking out at the gardens, I didn't feel right. Something was *off*. But I wasn't willing to yield. *She'll be right.*

Cut to the next scene, and I found myself standing at the end of an aisle in Bunnings, Thornleigh. A hazy, greyscale picture of the world had started to descend. My faint headache was now pounding, each heartbeat a merciless throb that threatened to pop a vein or two. Then the room started to spin gently. Instinctively, I grabbed the shelving, and my chest began constricting like it was caught in one of the vices for sale in aisle ten. As for my breathing, well, that was all over the place. Shallow. Mild panting. Then came the sweaty hands and the sudden realisation that my bowels were not okay either. This was about to get messy, in a very embarrassing and publicly shameful way.

Abandoning my trolley, I stumbled towards the exit. Two thoughts came to mind.

This wasn't the plan!

I have to get out of here now.

The idea of collapsing on the cold, hard floor at Bunnings and making a public spectacle of myself was more than I could bear.

Now, what followed was definitely one of the dodgier decisions this responsible first child had ever made. I don't remember how I did it, but I drove home. It took every last ounce of willpower, determination and bowel control I could muster. Shocking, mystifying and unlike anything else I'd experienced. Remember, I was the bloke who rarely got sick or had medical issues.

The next scene that unfolded was equally dramatic.

Bursting through the front door, I screamed Heather's name and stumbled towards the closest bed, which happened to be in our guest room. "My head! My head!" I screamed and cried in panic. I was burning up as I forced my palms into my temples. Tears were streaming, and I could barely breathe.

"What's going on?!" I said a few times as Heather tried to figure out why I was completely losing it.

Shooing the kids away, she quickly found icepacks and piled them on my burning head. I ended up going through a few of them.

It felt like I could literally see myself, as if I were positioned outside of my body as it writhed in pain. *Am I ... dying?*

Up next came the good ol' brown paper bag. Heather, always great in moments like this, held it over my mouth just like you see in the movies. I didn't think it would do anything, to be honest. But I was in acute pain, and I welcomed anything that could possibly help. And besides, now wasn't exactly the right moment to have a chat about her methods. Fortunately, the intervention did work, and I began to calm down.

I eventually passed out on that bed, sleeping for 7 hours in the middle of the day – rousing briefly before going on to sleep all night.

So, what was all the fuss about?

The whole experience felt surreal and way too dramatic. This wasn't part of my story. Other people had problems like this. Not me, or so I thought.

Panic attacks, I learnt weeks later, can look and feel like this. A strange mixture of uncontrollable fear and anxiety, utter confusion and an unbearable headache – like your head is going to explode. Honestly, I wanted to step outside of my own body to escape the pain, which is a bizarre thing to say.

The triggers that set off panic attacks are random. They don't care if it's Saturday and you've got a mindful day of gardening planned. In my case, the panic attack was a wake-up call. A proper turning point in my life.

My doctor examined me weeks later and said words I'll never forget. "Most men come to see me when they've crashed into the proverbial tree, but you've come to me just before you hit it."

To borrow the title of Bessel van der Kolk's book, the body keeps the score, and years of living with unchecked stress, fear and anxiety as a business owner finally caught up with me. I was worried about finances, our house, our family and what the future might hold. *Are our dreams for the future coming apart?* I didn't know it, but I was clinically depressed. Physically, mentally and emotionally unwell.

It turns out, your body just can't keep ploughing on as if everything is okay when it's clearly not. As a Gen Xer who grew up with *Star Wars*, I started to think of this as my Yoda moment.

"Fear is the path to the dark side. Fear leads to anger.
Anger leads to hate. Hate leads to suffering."
– Yoda

To be fair, I wasn't living with hate, but you get the point. My body was done pretending it was okay.

So, there we have it. The day my expectations about life came crashing down.

Saturdays would be forever different. My subconscious narrative was exposed – a life marked by the expectation of constant growth completely shattered by the hard reality of a human body not designed to live with stress indefinitely. As a middle-aged white bloke, it felt like a cliché. Even more jarring given I owned a sporty red convertible Mini with racing stripes – ironically, my joyful attempt at avoiding a midlife crisis.

Six years later, I'm thrilled to report I'm doing well.

Years of therapy, exercise, better food, improved sleeping routines and rewriting my inner narrative have done the trick. Imagine this. I can walk through busy shopping centres without triggering a fight-or-flight response! I've recaptured hope for the future, recovered my energy and developed an exciting vision for inspiring and equipping people to take a healthier path through life's travails. All possible because I've done hard personal development work to understand how I see myself in the world. Essentially, I deciphered the Story Code. Now I'm here to help you do the same.

YOUR NEW STORY STARTS NOW

Picture a middle-aged English bloke staring blankly out the window of a plane as it descends through the clouds. It's minutes before touchdown in Sydney after a long international flight from London. The man in question is British author Bill Bryson who wrote the 2000 classic *In a Sunburned Country*. "Flying into Australia, I realised with a sigh that I had forgotten again who their Prime Minister is… My thinking is that there ought to be one person outside Australia who knows."[1]

I love those lines – they're funny because it's true. We Aussies live with a grand national narrative. We're a little too self-important, if I'm honest. We enjoy a global reputation that betrays our population size of circa 27 million people. Our leaders strut around on the world stage, and yet our *entire nation* is just a bit bigger than the city of Dhaka, Bangladesh (24 million) and slightly smaller than Shanghai, China (30 million).[2]

Turns out, Bill's right. Historically, other countries have struggled to remember the names of our leaders. Even those of us who live here struggle to remember the name of our local politician. I reckon that's because other things are more important. Family, friends, sports teams, work, holidays. Lifestyle stuff. The good and the bad. We all share a version of this grand Australian narrative, as do people in other countries. We tell ourselves stories about what it means to live and work here. We're a wealthy nation that doesn't have many of the problems experienced by corrupt, war-torn countries. And we've got a picture in our heads about who we are and what we're becoming. While some of us are optimistic, many of us see the world darkly. Cost of living, stress, loneliness and burnout top the list of common problems.

This is a book about moments in time like Bryson staring out of a plane. Or perhaps for you it's staring out of a bus window, blank, burnt out and wondering why you're full of self-doubt. *Surely, there's more to life than this.*

As humans, we're constantly stitching together moments in time that help us make sense of it all. We're consciously and subconsciously telling ourselves stories about who we are and what we're doing. Some of us, like Bryson, are metaphorically staring at the world through a plane window – big-picture observers of strange cultures and tribes. Others of us are down on the ground, deep in the weeds. We feel life more deeply and intimately. We're changemakers, entrepreneurs, leaders and experts doing our bit to make the world a little better.

But as we'll discuss, we're at a social, cultural and technological inflection point. At this point in history, big-picture thinkers and detailed doers share a common trait – a growing disconnect between how we think life *should* go and how it's *really* going. It's a crisis born of the global polycrisis – multiple existential narratives that are transforming what we think about the future of our planet, people and daily lives. Western living has, until recent decades, delivered health, wealth and prosperity in the post-World War II years.

But now it's clear that accelerating geopolitics, AI-driven

technology, self-centred consumerism and climate are changing everything. They're impacting daily life, and for those who connect the dots between these macro trends, it's beyond alarming.

THE GOOD NEWS

The good news is there's always a way forward, even when it feels impossible. I've been there, done that and bought the souvenirs. Ever the ideas man, I had a couple of big aha moments that led to the research, interviews and writing that culminated in this book.

The first one was a simple process of reflection. *What if I could share my story and my storytelling insights with others? Maybe that could help leaders and working professionals transform their lives.* I realised the same storytelling techniques I teach leaders to grow their businesses helped me, and they can also be used to help people on their journeys. I think of it like standing in front of a window. Under the right lighting conditions, you can see the view outside *and* see yourself in the reflection – it's just a question of intentionally shifting your focus.

The other big aha was that I'm really not alone. Conventional wisdom dictates we feel much better when we know our difficult experiences aren't just our own. I'm not alone. Neither are you.

If you're someone who's experiencing some form of

self-doubt, career crisis, burnout or mental health related issue, this book is for you. It's written primarily for leaders, working professionals and high performers who feel stuck or held back by the stories they tell themselves. Overwhelmed, tired and burnt out. Self-doubt barely beneath the surface of everyday life. If that's you, my aim is to guide and inspire you in a practical and transformational way that's completely and uniquely relevant to your own story. Or maybe you're hyperaware of these issues and keen to avoid trouble. In truth, *everyone* can benefit from understanding the Story Code, so regardless of where you are in life, this book is for you.

Digging deeper, I've also written *The Story Code* with a few specific groups in mind.

LEADERS OF ORGANISATION OR TEAMS

You're doing well but feel unfulfilled, discontent or can't shake the self-doubt. You might even be staring burnout in the face. You'd like to stop the negative self-talk and, given the option, get rid of impostor syndrome (AKA impostor phenomenon) once and for all.

MID-CAREER PROFESSIONALS

You're talented, on the up, and have no shortage of opportunities. You're working hard, but it really is hard. Self-doubt, burnout and worries about the future are overwhelming. You're starting to lose that spark you once had years ago.

HUMAN RESOURCES, SALES AND MARKETING LEADERS

A leader in your own right, you could be facing the double whammy: identifying with these issues yourself while also being responsible for teams. There's a lot at stake, and you can't afford to slow down!

This book will also appeal to almost everyone in the workforce – entrepreneurs, the self-employed and other workers looking for the right way forward. Working life has never been so complicated! If only you had more clarity and confidence.

DECIPHERING THE STORY CODE

At its core, the Story Code is a transformational process that helps leaders rewrite their personal and professional stories. It unlocks hope, belonging and a sense of agency for leaders who feel stuck, overwhelmed or burnt out. When you master the Story Code, you master your life. Your relationships – both personal and professional – improve, and you meet each day with a healthy mindset, a clear purpose and a drive to succeed.

The Story Code comprises four key segments:

CHALLENGE

Name the dragon - meet your inner critic and uncover limiting beliefs.

OVERWRITE

Reframe meaning - script your new lead character.

DECIDE

Make a decision - rewrite your story.

ENCODE

Develop healthy habits for life - change everything with your new story.

To give you a complete understanding of the Story Code and what it can unlock, we'll decipher each segment further in chapter three.

My hope is that in these pages you'll find at least one great idea that will take you on the journey from self-doubt to self-belief, from feeling like you're barely surviving to thriving. The good news is, the first step doesn't always have to be a turning point or crisis like mine. The key to moving forward is paying attention to the stories you're telling yourself right now. Today. In the moment.

Not every day can be your ideal Saturday. But it is possible to master the Story Code, change the direction of your life and start writing a new story that applies to every day of the week.

Let's get into it.

THE POWER OF STORY

"We are not bound by the past; we are bound by the meaning we assign to it. Change the meaning, change the story."

IVANA MILOJEVIĆ

I've spent nearly 3 decades working as a professional storyteller. In various roles as a journalist, business leader, marketer and keynote speaker, I've earned a living helping leaders and organisations of all sorts write, tell and publish stories. I've studied marketing, communications and – *cue surprise!* – theology. That's right. In 2007, I left the media to study a Bachelor of Ministry.

I've always been fascinated with big-picture stories, hyper-local stories, mythologies, belief systems and everything in between. I'm a big fan of documentary makers like David Attenborough, Jane Goodall and Michael Moore – they possess a rare ability to see the big picture and small details at the same time. I'm no documentary maker, but I've written large slabs of content for newspapers, magazines, online and in social media over the years. My first book, *Beliefonomics: Realise the True Value of Your Story*, is a big part of my story – the beginning of a journey where I went from writing exclusively about others to bringing myself into the picture. The invisible wall between my professional self as the objective reporter faded, and the storyteller became part of the story.

Beliefonomics was published in 2020 – and it wasn't great timing. The COVID-19 pandemic poured cold water all over my book marketing ambitions. Regardless, *Beliefonomics* remains a gift that keeps on giving. A source of inspiration and practical tools that help storytellers shift from facts and figures to feelings.

You see, as a storyteller first in journalism and then corporate marketing, my work was mostly driven by experience, intuition and the joy of discovery. The missing gap fuelling *Beliefonomics* was a big question that, in my mind, needed answering: *What's the heartbeat of storytelling?* Answer: our worldviews and belief systems are profoundly shaped by the stories we're told. It's an idea that, curiously enough, was sparked not from my time in the media, but during my biblical studies. I discovered research that points to the fact our beliefs aren't fixed; they change over time thanks to storytelling. It was one of many new ideas I didn't expect to encounter on this grand new adventure.

As I studied counselling, psychology and the way our belief systems work (regardless of our personal faith or political outlook), I was challenged to reset my identity. My work in journalism *was* my identity. I was a *journalist*. It wasn't just a job. It was a filter through which I saw the world.

Unfortunately, years of cynically analysing people, products and companies had taken its toll. This fun, happy, stable and optimistic guy had started to lose his mojo and become jaded. Journalists are forever wary of people and companies. Most people lie, omit failures and hype small wins in an effort to earn valuable column inches.

The unforgettable turning point came when my ever-insightful wife saw my tired, sorry state and said, "I miss the old Mark." It was devastating because she was right. I knew I was unhappy about my cynical self, but I hadn't admitted the impact it was also having on those I loved.

What happened next? Well, my side hustle to earn money while studying was, you guessed it, writing and storytelling for the media and corporate clients. My little blog called *Filtered* became a company called Filtered Media. Heather and I accidentally started a storytelling and PR agency, and the rest, as they say, is history.

Through it all, my identity, sense of self-worth and ideas about the future began to shift. I no longer saw myself exclusively through a journalistic lens, nor an entrepreneurial one. My faith underwent a personal renaissance, and it was surprising to realise the life of a pastor in a small suburban church wasn't for me.

As our little agency grew from a few desks in our basement to a small office above a liquor shop in Wahroonga and then to fancy offices in Chatswood, my inner story changed. Yes, I was a storyteller, but that was what I *did*. It wasn't necessarily who I was. I realised I'm an encourager, a visionary who brings big ideas to life and loves to connect the dots. And boy do I love learning. Discovering that strength helped explain why I was so geekily obsessed with documentaries.

As these self-revelations emerged, I started rewriting my story in a series of notes on my iPhone. To this day, I'm constantly feeding new ideas, reflections and snippets of life into reasonably well-organised folders in my Notes app. I'm a digital bower bird, collecting fascinating bits of data throughout the day, just because I can. I'm interested, curious about new ideas, and I instinctively save stories for later. It's not perfect, and it's not a template for how you should live. It's just how I work. Curating ideas, making sense of people and events.

The most recent personality assessment I completed was Patrick Lencioni's 6 Types of Working Genius. His test says I'm a 'creative dreamer'. Someone who combines the attributes of invention and wonder:

> People with this pairing derive real joy and energy from contemplating the world around them and generating a fountain of new ideas. Generally idealistic and future-oriented, they are passionate about new possibilities that break through unnecessary boundaries. They don't value practicality, focus or implementation as much as idealism and ingenuity. This sometimes leads to stress or chaos among people around them who might be looking for realism and actionability.[1]

Yep, pretty much checks out. I love the freedom of creating and inventing with few constraints – and it's awesome when people ask me what I've been working on or thinking about: "Oh, well, here's something I prepared earlier!"

Now, I tell you all this because it gives you a sense of how, as someone who's made a living from storytelling, I've been re-writing my story. It's a strange process to go back and condense years of struggle, adventure and breakthrough. But, wow, is it worth it! With each aha moment, I've been propelled onwards. For example, I discovered that the difference between me succeeding on stage or not was the level of energy I brought into the room.

The scene was a small room at NIDA (National Institute of Dramatic Art) where I was doing a short course on speaking and stagecraft. It's a snapshot moment in my brain. I'd just delivered a 3-minute speech with all the earnestness I could muster. "How was that?" I asked with hesitation.

"It's good, but you need more energy."

The energy I thought I was bringing to the moment wasn't enough to impress my teacher. And she was right. I had more in the tank, and the next run at my mini performance un-locked a change in me I've carried for years.

To this day, I'm not short of energy on stage, in workshops or when hosting podcasts. I've learnt how to 'turn on the en-ergy', and it has become one of the stories I tell myself. Even if I'm unwell, not feeling great or simply hangry, I can still turn it on and make things happen because I know it's in there somewhere. Even better, I've discovered I'm at my best when I'm sharing that energy with others. Encouraging, building, giving, laughing and being funny – in my own mind, at least.

The flipside is a story that's common among comedians,

artists and other creatives. They often have a dark side. In the weeks, months and years that followed my 2019 panic attack, I sunk into the depths of a dark depression. I didn't want to accept the new, unfolding story. I didn't want it to become part of my identity. And yet, there it was. Facing that reality and reluctantly leaning into the healing process gave me back my energy.

Those of us in the content game know *how* to create compelling stories. I wanted to know *why* some stories worked and others didn't. Around 3 years of reading, research and pondering on the treadmill led to a revelation that stories do, in fact, change the world. The key was thinking less about the rational reasons we tell stories and diving deep into why stories that combine hearts and minds, emotions and logic, make all the difference.

An outsized emphasis on emotions plus a deep understanding of the belief systems among our target audiences can positively change lives and entire organisations.

It's a lesson many corporate, non-profit and government leaders are still discovering. There remains a myth that fact, figures and data alone drive our behaviour in response to stories, marketing and public messaging. You see this all the time in consumer advertising. The subtext isn't all that subtle: "Buy my product, it's only $9.99!" But that doesn't work for every organisation, particularly those in B2B and professional services where emotions and psychographics play an outsized role in our decision-making.

Through lots of research and reflection, I learnt that my story wasn't predetermined, fixed or outside my control. The storyteller became the story, and now I want to help you crack the Story Code. Some of us just survive, but it's way better to thrive.

CRACKING THE STORY CODE

I'm unashamedly optimistic because I believe the stories we tell ourselves change our lives. I dare to believe that these inner narratives are the missing link in a long line of remedies, therapies and exercises designed to help us navigate our personal and professional lives.

As you flick through the pages of *The Story Code*, you'll learn how we understand and rewrite the stories that define and transform our lives. Rewriting your story truly is an opportunity to break free from self-doubt and limiting beliefs, tame your inner critic and start realising *success* on your terms.

In my life, my work and my research, I've developed a profound understanding of how we can reflect on and rewrite the meaning attached to these moments in time I'm talking about. I've dug through a large body of research that draws a fascinating connection between our beliefs, the stories we tell ourselves and our long-term health and wellbeing outcomes. I've discovered that positive beliefs about our lives, including optimism and self-belief, are linked to resilience in the face of illness and stressful events. People choosing to focus on these traits tend to live healthier lifestyles and have better coping mechanisms.[2]

Fostering positive beliefs found in spirituality and religion tend to correlate with mental wellbeing and life satisfaction. That is, the stories we tell ourselves based on these healthy beliefs give us a framework for coping and meaning, and a sense of purpose.[3]

Storytelling itself is more than a communication tool we use to engage with other people, or to manipulate others in marketing and sales environments on behalf of our employer. Stories help us make sense of the world. They profoundly influence our sense of personal identity. They're vital for navigating hardships and finding hope.[4]

In fact, if we go right back to the ancient thinkers and philosophers, we discover a curious tension. As I touched on before, there's a modern myth that our beliefs, stories and feelings are fixed – people don't change. Our internal narratives rarely change. We're either left or right. Destinies are set, and you should probably just sigh and get on with it. An old friend of mine used to live by the motto: "Shut up and suffer!" But here's the thing: you don't always have to feel anxious. You won't always lack confidence. *I'm anxious* and *I'm unconfident* are examples of stories we tell ourselves. Stories we can rewrite.

Aristotle famously articulated this idea that we become what we repeatedly do: "Moral excellence comes about as a result of habit." Epictetus, one of the stoics, also has a great line: "Men [people] are disturbed not by things, but by the views which they take of them."

Then when we jump forward to the 20th century, narrative psychologists like Jerome Bruner and Dan McAdams made this idea even more explicit – our identity is a story we construct. Moreover, it's an ongoing process. As Bruner says, "Self is a perpetually rewritten story."[5] McAdams shares a similar idea: "People construct identity by integrating their life experiences into internalized, evolving life stories."[6] In short, each of us has a narrative identity whether we realise it or not. A personalised, internalised evolving story about our lives that wraps together the past, present and future.

Here's the key – the *big why*. The degree to which we find meaning and purpose within these stories of our lives – the suffering and adversity, the joys and triumphs – is the degree to which we can enjoy higher levels of mental health, wellbeing and maturity.[7] And if ever there was a time when more of us needed mentally healthier lives and a greater sense of wellbeing, it's now.

Life feels like it's getting progressively harder, not easier. In the 12 months I researched this book, I spoke with dozens of mid-career professionals about their experiences and discovered a universal sentiment.

**We're keeping it together – just –
but we're not thriving.**

The data backs up their experiences. Loneliness, mental health and burnout are on the rise in Australia and many Western nations.

Globally, 48 percent of 11,000 desk-based and frontline workers surveyed in Australia, Canada, France, Germany, India, Japan, UK and US were wrestling with burnout in 2024 – that's basically half of us![8]

Two key pieces of legislation are very public recognition that Australia is one of many countries that are starting to take this seriously. Through the *Fair Work Act 2009*, we've enshrined the 'right to disconnect' outside of regular working hours without penalty.[9] We need more downtime, more clarity and a greater sense of agency in our lives. Additionally, most of us are hungry for a greater sense of meaning at work.

Then we've got new work health and safety (WHS) regulations that, as of 1 April 2023, require employers to manage psychosocial risks to protect workers' mental health, improve worker retention and increase productivity. A code of practice developed by SafeWork NSW highlights areas that may cause harm to workers, including job design and management, hazardous equipment and environments, and of course social factors like workplace relationships.[10]

Beyond the complexities of maintaining compliant workplaces, the kicker for company directors and business owners is, of course, all this represents a new, growing risk – failure to comply will cost you money.

According to Safe Work Australia's prosecutions dashboard, across all WHS categories, 1,373 prosecutions and $164.22 million in penalties were recorded between 2020 and 2024. The average penalty was $122,920.[11] Not a lot of money in the scheme of things, but we're just getting started.

In 2025, mental health conditions were behind 9 percent of serious workers' compensation claims, a number that continues to rise. The kicker is those recovering from psychological injuries were off work for a median 34 weeks – four times longer than physical injuries.[12] Extended leave leads to compounding costs, lost productivity and overall risks.

Other nations are experiencing similar trends. Globally, the World Health Organization estimates the productivity cost of poor mental health sits at around US$1 trillion and 12 billion working days each year – and that's not counting court costs.[13] Big numbers – and there's more.

We're also seeing a surge in research exploring mental health and our inner narratives in the workplace and at home, and this issue's impact on the community. Academics talk about our collective hunger for meaning, clarity and a sense of coherence.

Amid all the noise, narrative therapy is one of the signals I've noticed. This form of psychotherapy helps us deal with change and reconstruct our identity around purpose and meaning. It's inspiring and exciting to dig into its unique power to transform lives, which we'll do in the chapters to come.

WHAT'S THE STORY? UNDERSTANDING THE PROBLEM

Outside the world of therapy, research and interventions, it has been interesting to watch how senior leaders in organisations across the world have stayed focused on mental wellness, professional development and psychosocial conditions. We're in the midst of a global shift in how we think and feel about our corporate leaders. They're more than bosses. They're holistic guardians of our working lives, and by extension partly responsible for our personal success in life. We're stacking both realistic and unrealistic expectations on our leaders and getting cranky when they don't meet our ever-shifting ideals.

A friend of mine, a senior leader at a multinational firm, quipped: "What if we just want to make money and run a successful business?" I mean, that's the basic job of a for-profit enterprise. He's got a point. But the trouble is, the rest of the world is moving on.

I've experienced this myself as a business owner and in my work with clients across five continents. Today, we tend to think about our workplace as the cornerstone of healthy living – leaders are required to be mindful of the way jobs impact the whole of a person's life. We don't have 'jobs' anymore. We have employment experiences, and they matter at a deeper level. And for additional drama, we're holding this expectation despite the existential threat posed by job-stealing AI platforms!

Marshall Goldsmith has a great line in his book *What Got You Here Won't Get You There* that brings some great colour and context to this problem:

> There's a reason I devote so much energy to identifying interpersonal challenges in successful people. It's because the higher you go, the more your problems are behavioral.[14]

The higher up the corporate or organisational ladder you climb, the more time you spend working on people problems. As I love saying from the stage, *it turns out people are difficult.*

So here's the drama in all its glory. The world needs healthy, happy, thriving leaders. And we the people want employers who care about us as fully formed, yet imperfect humans. It's an impossible situation, don't you think?

For starters, we tend to underinvest in teaching leaders

how to lead. Emotional intelligence is still regarded by old-school managers as a 'soft skill'. We love promoting people because they're good at working. For example, you could be great at sales, marketing, engineering, technology or finance. You do great technical work, so you get promoted. It's how the system works.

Then one day – *hey presto!* You're the boss.

I first clocked this idea when I was working in the media as a journalist and editor. It dawned on me that some journos didn't automatically become great leaders just because they were now the boss. In fact, it was often the case that brilliant writers were terrible at managing people. It's a great unspoken truth that many journalists are raging introverts. Not exactly the right make-up for inclusive, caring leadership.

I love the old saying that people often get promoted into *incompetence.* And that's particularly true in the media, arts and communications sector where we underinvest in leadership training. No doubt it's also true in many other sectors.

The not-for-profit sector is ironically another one. One study found that 58 percent of 220 charities surveyed prioritised the needs of their clients and communities instead of investing in their teams and volunteers.[15] It followed a survey from a few years prior that found nearly half of social sector workers are stressed or anxious "often or always." They're also frustrated, cynical or exhausted, again, "often or always."[16] Turns out, servant-hearted people often put themselves last, to their detriment.

It leads to a question I've been asking myself against this backdrop: *How can we expect leaders to understand the deep needs, wants and motivations of their teams without first understanding their own?* And so, we get to another question: Why does the Story Code matter in our professional journeys?

Our old mate Aristotle comes to the party with another famous quote and the beginning of an answer: "He who cannot be a good follower cannot be a good leader." Wise decisions tend to come from leaders with strong characters who understand their desires, emotions and habits. They've mastered the Story Code.

LEAD YOURSELF FIRST

We already know the foundations of a healthy, balanced life: good food, proper sleep, and exercise. They're fundamental pillars for surviving and thriving over time. Each one is essential and well-researched, and the best practices are largely understood. And importantly, each one is completely within our control.

I believe organisations and leaders are at risk of overlooking the fourth pillar necessary to survive and thrive in the 2020s and beyond – *how we manage our mindsets through the stories we tell ourselves.* Now, more than ever, the psychosocial aspect of working life needs maximum attention.

Now, to be fair, this is also a well-researched topic. Way back in 1952, Norman Vincent Peale gave us *The Power of Positive Thinking*. Then we've got Stephen Covey's classic, *The 7 Habits of Highly Effective People*, and my personal favourite, Carol Dweck's *Mindset: The New Psychology of Success*. You won't have trouble finding many, many more books, research papers and articles on the topic. Yet not many talk in detail about how we can rewrite the stories we tell ourselves (yes, I've checked!), despite the fact it's part of our default human programming. It's worth thinking about our inner storytelling through the lens of experts in narrative therapy.

In his book on narrative therapy, *Retelling the Stories of Our Lives*, David Denborough discusses a person he worked with called 'Vanessa' (not her real name). The story she told herself, tragically, was that she was "good for nothing."[17] Using a series of crosses and simple lines, he depicts how this story evolved over time, drawing a thread between key moments in Vanessa's life. Her ex-husband's abuse, her ex-husband's taunts, the moment she lost her apartment, and the stress of moving to a new place and paying rent.[18] Each one is a snapshot of a key moment in time. No doubt Vanessa can tell you in detail how she felt in each of those moments. Describe the room in detail. Where she stood and what she said to herself in each of those moments.

Denborough says Vanessa is experiencing a type of confirmation bias. Each snapshot is a moment in time that reinforces the story she's been telling herself – she's "good for nothing."[19] This is a person who's given up on believing she can have a better future. She lacks self-confidence and self-esteem. You can imagine her saying, "See! Look at the evidence. I really am good for nothing."

Denborough goes on to explain the bigger picture. In any culture, we form a dominant belief system or story about what it means to be a worthy person. In the West, we value being self-possessed and self-contained. Highly productive, useful people who are individuals at the expense of community and independent at the expense of connection (no wonder we're lonely and burnt out!).[20] Some find it easy to conform and meet these expectations. Others struggle to fit into these cultural norms or fail to meet their own unrealistic expectations. They end up feeling like outsiders and less valuable. The culture's belief system has failed them.

People like Vanessa are only part of this story. High achievers, perfectionists and leaders of all stripes are vulnerable to burnout, depression and the stress that comes from fighting our own inner narratives in a time-poor world that seems to value entertainment more than meaningful ideas. And so self-judgement kicks in when these leaders do well, earn praise or find themselves tempted to think they're a 'good person'.

Each of us has an inner critic that pops up instantly in these moments:

- *You're not doing* that *well!*

- *You were just* lucky *on that project.*
- *Of course you're not a good person.*
- *Think about all the bad things you've said about those people at work!*

It's brutal. We're so selective about the stories we stitch together about ourselves in our minds. We're so focused on the negative, demoralising inner narratives that we drag ourselves down. There's a popular saying that applies here: if we treated our friends the way we treat ourselves, we'd have no friends at all!

OUR OWN STORIES MATTER

It's time we called ourselves out. It's time we brought these subconscious, destructive stories into the light. Because the stories we tell ourselves are the narratives that run our lives.[21] They're the inner voice and personal narrative that profoundly shape every aspect of the way we live our lives. These stories act like a filter on a smartphone video – sometimes we're using a positive filter to feel good about what we're seeing, but most of the time it's a dark, grainy filter.

Here's the challenging idea: you are the master storyteller of your own life, so you get to decide what events in your life mean. And most importantly, you alone have the power to re-author your story in a deeply personal and meaningful way. It isn't anyone else's responsibility, and they shouldn't be shaping it unless you've decided to accept their advice.

The only catch, and it's a big one, is that you also have to believe in yourself. You're an audience of one, and you know when you're lying. I've rewritten my story a few times over, and to be truly, brutally honest, self-belief is one of the hardest roads to tread on this journey from surviving to thriving.

Here's a tragic example from the world of heavy-metal music. My teenage years were a haze of stonewashed jeans, ten-holed Dr Martens boots and flannel shirts worn while I played in hard-rock bands, so stay with me.

You might know about Megadeth, an iconic band formed in the 1980s. To this day, it's considered one of the 'big four' metal bands alongside Metallica, Anthrax and Slayer.

There's a famous story about Dave Mustaine, Megadeth's founder, who formed the group after he was kicked out of Metallica in 1983.[22] This was a massive moment in rock music history. Now, despite all the drama that has played out in the tension between Megadeth and Metallica over the past 40 years, Mustaine went on to sell more than 15 million records and become an icon in his own right. He should be happy, right? Sadly, no. He doesn't carry a success story in his heart and mind.

Speaking to Metallica drummer Lars Ulrich in the 2004 documentary *Metallica: Some Kind of Monster*, a tearful Mustaine said the departure ruined his life for the following

20 years. People hated him because he "wasn't good enough" for Metallica. "Am I happy being number two? No." Ulrich, admitting feelings of guilt, said he found it difficult to comprehend why Mustaine's dominant life story was rooted in that one event.[23] The simple explanation is that he was trapped in a victim mindset – we'll talk about this type of narrative shortly.

Mustaine's story illustrates why it's critical you understand what it means to be the master storyteller of your own life. Each of us can choose to rewrite our personal narratives in honest, meaningful ways that define success on our terms. After all, nobody else is going to write your story for you, unless you let them.

In Mustaine's case, it's not too late. He could still choose to write a new story that recognises the world wouldn't have his music without that life-defining moment. He could also choose to be content with the financial success, lifestyle and fame that have come from decades of hard work.

Now, I've never been a music journalist, but I have interviewed thousands of business, technology and political leaders over the years. I've met leaders who reflect a sense of calm confidence. They understand what's going on around them and even during hard times can think clearly about the way forward. And I've seen the Mustaine story before. Impostor phenomenon, self-criticism, fears, doubts, burnout and worries are corrosive. So many of us wear masks, hoping to cover up any perceived inadequacies in the stories we tell ourselves.

We want to keep those stories on the inside and tell the world something else. It also manifests in another tragic way.

People suffering from self-doubt and burnout can't move forward. In fact, they're holding themselves back from letting go and jumping headlong into all the world has to offer. It's like they're gripping the handbrake tightly, holding it up and refusing to let go.

Sound like you? Maybe you're holding yourself back because there's a story running through your head about failure, lack or burnout. But what if there's a big idea that the world needs? A new company, product, service or creative expression. Or maybe a different company out there needs you! There's nothing quite like the stress of holding the handbrake for months and years on end. Afraid to change, face your fears and let go. I've been there.

If that sounds like you too, let me suggest it's time to begin the journey from barely surviving to thriving. It's time to master the Story Code and rewrite your story – and I'd love to show you how.

CHAPTER 2

PROBLEMS, PROBLEMS, AND MORE PROBLEMS

"The world feels way out of control, and it's squeezing the life out of us."

Before we can embrace the solution, we must understand the problems we're facing – and in modern life, there are *bucketloads*.

The world is getting a little crazy, don't you think? We're witnessing some incredible events, from wars, famine and political violence to environmental disasters. Through it all, our news feeds are packed with the quotes and stories told by national leaders seeking to direct public narratives in their favour. It has always been thus. Entire nations and communities rise and fall on the strength of storytelling – for better or worse. Storytelling always has been, and always will be, enormously powerful and equally mystifying.

But it's not just the macro narratives that matter. The stories we tell ourselves matter too. Stories that often go unchecked, unfiltered and misunderstood. Think about it like this. Our eyes, ears and brains work together like a smartphone in video recording mode. They're busy recording everything, all the time. And occasionally, our brains take a photo or screenshot at the same time. Every single person on this stunning third rock from the sun is consciously or subconsciously writing the stories of their lives in this way. Snapshots of moments in time, both good and bad, that live in our hearts and minds. They're events, words and feelings that are a bit like the photos in your smartphone. If we keep scrolling back, our memories stretch way into history.

The stories we tell ourselves help us make sense of the world. Stories create meaning. They shape our identity and form the foundations of daily life.

I was deeply moved by the story of Dr Kylie Moore-Gilbert who spoke at Social Impact Summit 2025, an event organised by a company I co-founded, ImpactInstitute. Kylie is an academic with expertise in Middle Eastern political science. She famously survived 804 days in two of Iran's worst jails.[1] Locked up on false charges of espionage while attending a conference, she became a pawn in the geopolitical game of prisoner swaps. Standing on stage, she spoke about a seminal moment in her small, isolated cell. Deprived of exposure to the outside world and human contact for 23 hours per day, you're faced with two choices: rage and scream, potentially driving yourself insane, or retreat back into a space inside your mind where you're utterly absorbed in the present moment. Allowing her thoughts to drift, Kylie went back into the deep recesses of her mind and discovered detailed memories of life at primary school. Walking through the corridors. Seeing the people and environment that, until then, she'd completely forgotten. Moments, images, pictures and feelings locked away in the recesses of her mind came back as she surrendered to the reality of her situation.

Very few of us, I trust and pray, will ever find ourselves experiencing that level of trauma. Yet it's a reminder of the enduring power of stories, events and moments in life. Our digital memory bank is storing those videos and pictures daily and at night when we dream. We're constantly flashing back to past moments and casting forward to what life will be like in the future. Incredible! Some of us enjoy picturing an entirely different life. Others feel doomed to repeat the tragic mistakes of our pasts. Stuck in an endless loop, victims of powers beyond our control.

DECIPHERING THE CURRENT CRISIS

It's no secret we're living in an era where mental wellbeing and dissatisfaction with working life are at crisis levels. At the mild end of the spectrum, few appreciate just how pervasive stress, self-doubt and impostor phenomenon are across the global workforce – and how much of a toll they're taking.

Incredibly, 7 in 10 women have experienced impostor phenomenon at least once in their careers. Around 25 percent experience these emotions often.[2] It's rarely a once-off experience across genders and ages. Once you start questioning your abilities, the questions rarely stop without intervention.

In 2024, a Headspace study found that 47 percent of those surveyed say most, or all, of their stress comes from work, and 71 percent say work-related stress caused a personal relationship to end.[3] Further, a Moodle study found that a disturbing two-thirds of US workers are experiencing burnout.[4] Figures vary, but one study estimated that burnout costs a company with 1,000 employees US$5 million each year.[5]

Then we've got the fact men and women have reported lower levels of life satisfaction since 1985.[6] Stress levels have kept rising for 30 years despite our collective obsession with mindfulness, fitness and eating well.[7] Since 1960, rates of depression have also been on the rise among young people and adults.[8] No doubt this is having a devastating impact on society.

Here in Australia, the story isn't any better. Our so-called 'lucky country' is becoming burnout nation. A 2022 study found that 64 percent of Australian workers experience burnout, *the highest of any country surveyed*. For comparison, the global average rate of burnout was around 40 percent.[9] That means a clear majority of Australian working professionals have been feeling burnt out for years.

But wait, it gets worse! Nearly 40 percent of Australian workers expected stress levels and burnout to increase in 2025 compared to the year prior. Two in five were already burnt out at the start of the year, and 90 percent believe burnout is largely ignored until it becomes critical.[10]

Then we have this incredible fact: Australian employees experience among the highest daily stress rates globally. Gallup found that 49 percent experience stress a lot of the day.[11] Our top three stressors? Job demands, leadership and psychological safety.[12] Fun times in the office! *Not*.

The implications for business leaders are obvious: more

people 'quietly quitting', poor employee retention, lower productivity and the spectre of costly psychosocial injury payouts.

At a personal level, we tend to talk about impacts such as
exhaustion and fatigue. But the less well-understood problem
is of course the stories we tell ourselves during times like this.
Stories like, *My life won't get better, I'm no good at this job* and,
I don't have what it takes. They're lines that tend to reinforce a
narrative that you're stuck and options are limited. I've been
there, and beyond the obvious trauma and suffering, it can feel
like a type of claustrophobia.

For others, there's a resonance with Mel Robbins's 'Let
Them Theory'. There's a tension that builds each day when
small things and random comments trigger you in unexpected
ways – crankiness and snappiness follow! Robbins' stake on
this borrows from the stoics. Let go of things you can't control and focus on what you can control – yourself. Feeling
triggered? "Let them." And then, "Let me …" It's no surprise
the idea is popular. 'Let them' is a simple, quick release from
stressful moments. Saying 'let me' (take action) shifts the focus
back to what you can do in the moment.[13] But is that enough?
It feels exhausting. Actually, I *know* it's exhausting to try and
maintain mental gymnastics like this all day long. You're not
treating the root causes of burnout, stress and self-doubt. In
fact, the research suggests that we really do have to go after
these root causes. Too many people are going to some very
dark places because their lifestyles aren't sustainable.

In Australia, there were 954 suspected or confirmed suicide deaths in 2024 – higher than the previous 3 years.[14] In the 12 months leading up to May 2025, 22 percent of Australians (4.3 million people) experienced a mental disorder, and 17 percent experienced an anxiety disorder.[15] That's 1 in 5 people at risk of causing harm to themselves and others.

Like my doctor explained, most people, especially men, don't see a doctor or talk to a friend before they hit the proverbial tree. In fact, approximately 75 percent of Australians who take their own lives are men, across all age groups. Roughly six every day.[16] Every single day.

Globally, the news is equally distressing. Depression impacts approximately 280 million people worldwide, while anxiety-related issues affect 301 million people.[17] It's shocking, I know. It's a tragedy of modern-day life that we live in an era of such incredible wealth, have access to so many opportunities and technologies, and yet so many people feel overwhelmed and depressed.

And yes, I know these stats are a tough start for what is ultimately a book about empowerment, hope and a positive way forward. The trouble is we're seeing real signs of existential crises in the basic fabric of what we think is a healthy, modern society. We're individualistic wealth accumulators struggling to find meaning in it all, across all demographics. This is an honest picture of our times, and it's about time we made it an even bigger priority than it already is. Too many people simply can't find a healthy way out of crisis, stress and negative mindsets.

As Bono might say, we still haven't found what we're looking for – and we're not happy about it.

THE CONTRAST BETWEEN THEN AND NOW

Go back a few decades, and life really was different. It's easy to forget the joy of living life in neat little boxes, each part of our lives separated from the other. In our minds, we had a box for work, a box for home, family, friends, sports, faith communities and so on. Men like me loved this approach to life because everything was organised and simple!

Today's reality couldn't be more jarring. Working from home, it's not unusual to plan meals, put a load of washing on between Zoom calls, chat with the kids and so on. This is of course the stuff of nightmares for people who love neat boxes or don't like being interrupted.

Then we've got the issue of job titles. Just 20 years ago, in my lived working experience, it seemed that professional titles mattered more than they do today. We turned up at work with a title hanging over our heads, mentally speaking. The goal was to keep moving up the ladder, collecting titles like little trophies as we lived the dream.

It was also a time when toxic masculinity, bullying and

unkindness were rampant, particularly in media, technology and business circles where I began climbing the career ladder. Psychosocial hazards? For many, that was normal life at work. Dodge unsafe people, play the game and try to keep your head above water – just like life in high school! It's baffling to look back in my mind's eye and wonder why we didn't make a bigger deal about it.

Now, you might say that nothing has changed, and perhaps that's true in some organisations. But the world of work really has been changing for the better since the #metoo movement took off in the wake of the Harvey Weinstein scandal in 2017. This man infamously used his power and privilege in Hollywood to gain sexual favours from aspiring female actors. It was a proper tipping point in the workplace. Psychosocial hazards were suddenly front and centre. Invisible stresses and mental torment became visible and – critically – no longer tolerable.

This too was, in my view, the moment when HR professionals faced a reckoning. No longer could they enjoy an exclusive focus on what mattered for the company. The experience of being at work climbed up the agenda. We started seeing more person-centred policies where fewer people were punished for speaking out. The seeds of the 4-day work week conversation were planted.

Another critical turning point in the workplace was the long-tail impact of the Black Lives Matter (BLM) movement in 2020. Equality at work and within society at large is still a hot topic, but the BLM movement paved the way for the normalisation of other topics such as gender and marriage equality, sustainability practices and the social impact of workplaces. In short, we woke up to the hardly radical idea that our experiences in the workplace directly influence our mental wellbeing, and in turn shape our home lives and the community at large.

SPEED IS AN ISSUE

Social progressives like me love this conversation. It's so encouraging to reflect on the ways we're becoming kinder, more tolerant and inclusive. And yet, the problem we're facing in the workplace now can easily feel like two steps forward, one step back.

As I write, the United States is dramatically retreating from its role as 'leader of the free world' and with that, there are serious downstream impacts in many Western countries. In the workplace, there's pressure to cut DEI (diversity, equity and inclusion) programs and retreat from conversations about social progress.

Likewise, artificial intelligence is a runaway freight train. It is without doubt the most transformative, disruptive and compelling tech-driven development in human history. Artificial general intelligence is on the near horizon, and just a little further down the track is a world where general purpose,

AI-powered robots will infiltrate every aspect of working and home life. To make matters even more frightening, nobody has any real ideas about how this will all play out.

Then we've got the speed of change. In 2024, I was hosting executive roundtables with C-suite leaders who were debating the merits of experimenting with generative AI. Twelve months later, they were building AI-driven workflows, deploying agents, and behind closed doors, actively considering how many of these agents will replace employees.

One of the first tech companies to catch my eye in early 2025 was Workday, which infamously sacked 1,750 people and replaced them with AI agents.[18] Others actively switching humans for AI agents include Cisco, UPS, Intuit, Duolingo and Klarna.[19] Then in more recent times, Microsoft, Atlassian and Canva have sparked news coverage for sacking thousands of people – stories that do nothing to assuage the feeling that AI is indeed out to eat your career.[20]

Finally, all these issues are turbocharged by an even larger, meta crisis of the mind – worries about environmental catastrophe, generational inequality and geopolitical instability. Technically speaking, it's a polycrisis – we're overwhelmed by multiple, interconnected crises that seem to be feeding each other.[21]

If we hold these ideas in tension and cast our minds back to the workplace, we're starting to see downstream impacts from this polycrisis.

1. We're Redefining Success

The very definition of what defines success is being rewritten. It's a profound issue for almost everyone in the workforce, particularly those of us in the middle and later stages of our careers.

When climbing the corporate ladder was the only game in town, it was very easy to measure success. But today, your definition of success could be achieving work-life balance, a short commute, lots of time with the kids, escaping the grind and working remotely, starting your own business or earning enough money to retire early. You might also want to solve one of the multiple global crises!

There's no single script or set of social expectations, and for some that's a daunting prospect.

2. Traditional Pathways Are Porous

Sometimes you really can have too many options. Younger generations see the world through a different lens because they're AI natives. They're surfing a digital wave that's chopping and changing all over the place. Some are creating AI startups; others are hustling with ecommerce sites, and almost everyone wants to be a millionaire YouTuber.

Traditional pathways from school to university, college or a trade are fuzzy. For example, I had to persuade my 16-year-old son to finish high school. Not because he's a bad student – on the contrary, he's rather sharp. So sharp he had this question: "Why should I keep learning when AI will just tell you the answer?"

We used to joke about entrepreneurs dropping out of university. Now the kids are looking critically at the value of *high school*.

My response? He still needs to learn the value of critical thinking and the difference between knowledge and wisdom. That got me over the line – for now!

3. The Boxes Have Vanished

The old neat boxes I was talking about have disappeared. The invisible barrier between our personal and professional lives is gone, and we *expect* to know about our colleagues' personal lives.

Perhaps the most visible example of this at scale is LinkedIn. There was a time on LinkedIn not so long ago when we were very careful with our emotions. We were "pleased to announce" we were starting a new job, discussing how "excited" we were.

Now we've recreated Facebook in our professional social network. Deeply personal stories and big family moments are making headlines. Authenticity? Maybe. Emotional vulnerability? Most definitely. And we're normalising conversations about how psychologically safe, or unsafe, we're feeling at work.

Shani Orgad, professor of media and communications at

the London School of Economics, calls this societal shift the "vulnerability turn." This turn began during the pandemic when people started writing the "snap" (breaking point) story. Here's how the narrative goes: a professional reaches breaking point, writes about their challenges, then goes on to describe the bold and challenging new life that lies ahead. Colour me guilty! At the same time, snap stories illustrate the mood of the times – working life feels like it's getting harder. More overwhelming. And we need to share our stories.

LOSING CONTROL

Think about all these issues we're identifying. Rapidly changing work experiences, technological transformation at hyper-speed and a relatively sudden outpouring of emotional vulnerabilities. And it's all being shared at scale for everyone to read.

American author and journalist Joan Didion was no stranger to reflecting on hard times and sharing her trauma with the world. "We tell ourselves stories in order to live," she wrote in her 1979 book *The White Album*.[22] That is, we're wired to try and make sense of life's big moments before we can move onwards. This existential crisis in the workplace is a bit like that. It's hard to get clarity and move forward in your career without a clear sense of what's going on around you.

At the local level, cost of living concerns and politics dominate corporate agendas. At national and international levels, it's hard to understand exactly what's going on in the world right now.

Boards and executive teams, once able to minimise the impact of geopolitical movements on daily operations, have in recent times been unable to separate them. I've spoken at conferences where leaders have told me in corridors that political concerns and global economic instability are destabilising entire organisations.

Five-year strategic plans? Forget it! Let's just get through the next quarter.

Stephen Covey's famous 'Circles of Concern, Influence and Control' tool is one of the best at our disposal for making sense of the mess.[23]

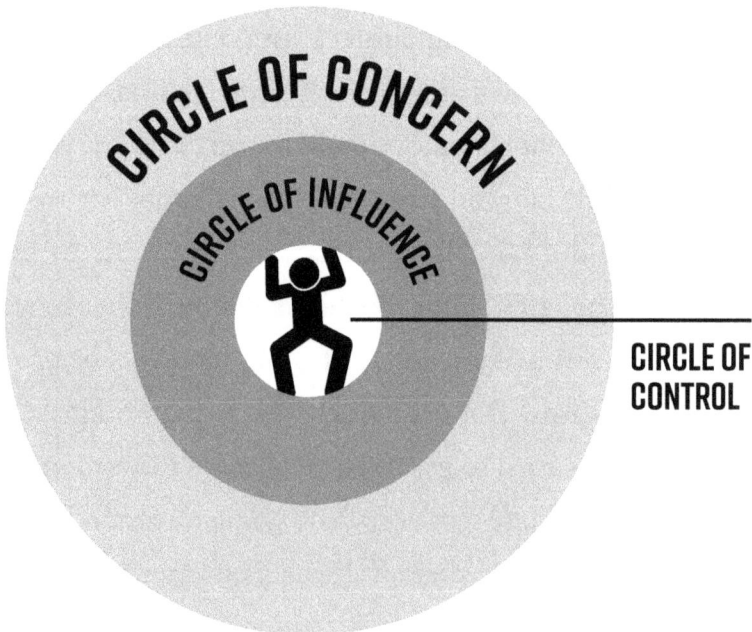

CIRCLE OF
CONTROL

In the middle, you can see the *Circle of Control* where each of us has agency and control over what we think and how we respond to the world. It's where our internal stories and conscience live. We tell ourselves stories about what we can and can't do on a daily, moment-to-moment basis.

Moving out, the *Circle of Influence* is where we can positively or negatively impact relationships and situations around us. Your work colleagues, clients, neighbours, family and moody baristas live here. Your behaviour and the stories you tell yourself directly influence how they live their lives, one way or the other.

Finally, we move out to the *Circle of Concern* where very few things are in our control. Better thought of as the *Circle of No Control*, this is the sphere of wars, poverty, environmental destruction and celebrity fashion shoots on the red carpet – I mean, what *are* they wearing these days?

I was reminded of this simple model during an internal workshop at ImpactInstitute. I had an aha moment because, in an instant, I realised many of the issues causing me to feel overwhelmed and out of control were indeed found inside the *Circle of No Control*. I'd started to believe a story I was telling myself about external forces having too much control over my life, and there wasn't much I could do about it. My daily news reading habits weren't helping. I'm a lifelong news hound and constant, always-on learner. I'd curated multiple streams of content across social sites and news apps, and they were starting to overwhelm me with negativity.

In one of many ironic, meta moments, I came across a quote from artist and performer Tim Minchin who was wrestling with the same problem. Speaking on the UK's Channel 4, he discussed quitting social media because it was affecting him personally:

> I found myself not okay in myself a lot because of how distressed I was, and so I just needed – it's not that I've buried my head in the sand – I just need to have agency in what I'm seeing and what I'm reading, and not let the algorithm tell me what I should be seeing and reading.[24]

Like me, Minchin was losing his sense of control. And there's a good chance you know what I'm talking about.

THE GREAT SQUEEZE

Feelings of overwhelm, stress, being out of control and simply *stuck* have always been part of the human experience. But as we discussed earlier, we're now at a point of crisis. Many of us in the world of work have crossed the threshold beyond normal daily stresses to an abnormal barrage of confusing inputs that make clear thinking nearly impossible. I've started calling it the *Great Squeeze*. Overwhelmed by so much negative news at speed, our Circles of Control and Influence are getting squeezed. It feels like we're losing agency over our lives. We're less able to positively influence others who are themselves caught up in the relentless internal chatter. If the voices in our heads stay too loud for too long, it's not unreasonable to fear they'll push us to an unhealthy place.

Here are a few examples of what's going on in the world that illustrate my point.

LYING FLAT

Remember reading about *lying flat*? For years, Chinese youth have been lying flat in response to relentless work and social pressures. Known in China as '*tan ping*', it no doubt upsets the Chinese government because these kids have rejected the '996' system – working 9 am to 9 pm, 6 days per week. They've basically given up. No personal ambition and a refusal to judge their lives by materialistic standards. They love minimalism.

In China, young workers are also leaving big cities and returning to regional areas to improve their lifestyles, which by my reckoning is a much better idea.

The Japanese have also taken on the world by lying down. A phenomenon called '*hikikomori*' describes a state of social withdrawal adopted in response to the pressures of the world. These modern-day hermits are nearly 1.5 million working-age people who rarely leave home, 60 per cent of which identify as male.[25]

Here in Australia and other English-speaking nations, it's less clear-cut, but we all know the big pressures impacting young and old. Rising house prices, the cost of living, social pressures and climate anxiety.

Again, looking at the experience of our kids as a barometer of hope for the future, I came across one rather telling comment on Reddit from a teacher:

> There is a large proportion of students who are
> lazy and apathetic about life in general these days.
> These students go from retail to retail job after high
> school and have little ambition for anything else.
> How do we address the needs of those students?[26]

It's not a one-off. At the time of writing, Heather and I have four children aged 22, 19, 16 and 11. They're not apathetic, but we're eagle-eyed observers of their peer groups. Once you look beyond the mullets, questionable fashion and odd use of the English language, it's remarkable to realise just how much underlying cynicism and stress is a normal part of their lives. Comparison culture and relentless social engagement dominate their lives. Snapchat streaks are a great example. One of my boys has kept up a streak (one message from each person once per day) for hundreds of days with his best friend – the equivalent of 4 years!

Technologies like this are subconsciously embedding

underlying stress and anxiety in their hearts and minds – don't break the streak! Don't miss a message!

REWIRING OUR BRAINS

So what impact is all this having on us as humans? Social media is, of course, the moral outrage of our time. TV, radio, music and printed media have all been accused of destroying the fabric of society. However, research suggests that social is a different beast to other media. Social media activates the same neurological pleasure circuits triggered by nicotine, alcohol and cocaine. Judith Edersheim, co-director of the Center for Law, Brain & Behavior at Harvard, says giving children access to social media and smartphones is like putting them in a 24-hour casino and giving them chocolate-flavoured bourbon. "The relentlessness, the intrusion, it's all very intentional. No other addictive device has ever been so pervasive."[27] Adults are equally impacted by social media, but of course we have the joy of adding it to all the other grown-up burdens.

Researchers at the University of Melbourne have been following the lives of 17,000 Australians each year over the course of their lifetimes. They found we Aussies have experienced increasing psychological distress during the past 15 years. The proportion of women living with psychological distress soared by around 63 per cent between 2007 and 2021. For men, that figure is a little lower at 51 per cent.[28]

Beyond the scarily high numbers, what's curious about this study is the starting point – 2007. That's the year when Facebook started to take off, clocking 50 million users that year.[29] Likewise, X (then Twitter) took off in 2007, and our old friend LinkedIn reached 10 million users in the same year.[30] Rounding out this banner year, late Apple co-founder Steve Jobs launched the iPhone on 29 June 2007 and kickstarted the transformational smartphone era.[31]

That means we're nearly 2 decades into a socio-technological experiment that's rewiring the human brain and changing the fabric of society. And no, I'm not being alarmist. Dr Ferdi Botha, a researcher involved in the University of Melbourne study I referenced, says smartphones continue to make us feel more disconnected. He says the combination of the COVID pandemic and extended periods of smartphone use has caused a rise in psychological distress, anxiousness and dissatisfaction, particularly among people aged 15 to 24.[32]

That's obviously not great news as we move towards a world where everyone except small babies and dogs has a smartphone (and even in those cases, we're still sticking tracking tags on them!). By 2026, 23.6 million Australians will be using a smartphone, and more than 90 percent of Australians between the ages of 12 and 55 already have a social media account.[33]

Hugh Mackay, Australia's much-loved social psychologist, is all over this idea too. He says we're more connected than ever, and yet more lonely, more anxious, more depressed, more medicated, more sleep-deprived, more gambling-addicted and more economically unequal.

> The most realistic way to interpret the fact that we, and comparable Western societies, are experiencing social fragmentation on such a large scale is to see it as a self-inflicted wound. We have created a culture of such radical individualism – where self-actualisation is regarded as our greatest accomplishment – that social fragmentation, with its heightened risk of social isolation, is the inevitable consequence.[34]

Keep in mind this is a man who has studied the Australian psyche since the mid 1950s. It's uplifting stuff, right? Well, for those of us in business and professional settings, it's no wonder issues like resilience, burnout, anxiety, stress and work-life balance dominate our conversations. Our inability to increase mental, physical and spiritual wellbeing impacts the way we handle stress and recover from tough times.[35] And of course, that flows through to our performance at work, collective productivity and the financial health of our organisations.

ANOTHER SERVING OF PROBLEMS

One way of thinking about all these problems is the expectations we all have about what it means to live and contribute to a healthy society. In most democratic societies, we expect upward mobility. Each generation should live better than the previous one. We want our kids to have better lives than ours, live on a healthier planet and do even more amazing things. How often have you heard experts on TV, in documentaries or in movies use the line: "One day your kids will ask you what you did about the climate crisis/social inequality/ wars/poverty?"

An expectation of upward mobility is also woven into the wealth narrative. We're currently in the midst of the largest transfer of intergenerational wealth in history – from baby boomers to gen Xers and millennials – some $3.5 trillion over the coming decades in Australia alone.[36] And yet extreme levels of inequality remain across the world. Trickle-down economics has largely failed, a point crystal clear in US politics as protesters and politicians rage against tax cuts for corporations and the ultra-rich. In fact, in the US, just three people own more wealth than the bottom half of American society.[37] Staggering! Adding insult to injury, the average American worker has the same purchasing power they did in 1978, all while the wealth gap widens.[38]

In my home country, the Australian Council of Social Service (ACOSS) reported that, in 2024, nearly half of all wealth was held by the highest 10 percent of households, worth an average of $5.2 million each. These households have 15 times the wealth of the lowest 60 percent.[39]

Meanwhile, the average wealth of an Australian household in the top 20 percent is $3.25 million – six times that of the middle 20 percent wealth group ($565,000) and over 90 times that of the lowest 20 percent wealth group ($36,000).[40]

But wait – there's more bad news! Globally, one-fifth of the world's wealthiest people now receive about 70 times the income of the poorest one-fifth.[41] And that ratio is getting worse over time.[42]

Here's a killer quote from Ha-Joon Chang, a South Korean economist:

> Once you realize that trickle-down economics does not work, you will see the excessive tax cuts for the rich as what they are – a simple upward redistribution of income, rather than a way to make all of us richer, as we were told.[43]

Then we've got Warren Buffett, who needs no introduction except to say that I don't know why he eats so much McDonalds:

> The rich are always going to say that you know, just give us the money and we'll go out and spend more and then it will all trickle down to the rest of

you. But that has not worked the last 10 years, and I hope the American public is catching on.[44]

FEELING ENCOURAGED YET?

It's all pretty gloomy stuff, hey?

The bottom line is most people are carrying a multitude of stresses. We're absorbing torrents of negative information on small screens, and for many of us, it feels like our Circle of Control keeps getting smaller.

Is there *anything* you can do to change the world and make it better? This is the *Great Squeeze* of our modern age. No wonder overall satisfaction with life in Australia is now at an all-time low. The *Australian Unity Wellbeing Index* found that average life satisfaction in the community dropped from a score of 85.2 percent in 2009 to 78.5 percent in late 2024. The sting in the tail? People under 55 have significantly lower levels of life satisfaction and higher levels of mental distress than older Australians.[45]

I've gotta say, I get it. Heather and I are sliding into our 50s and have four kids. Raising kids in your 30s and 40s is proper hard work. You're raising a family, working hard; there's financial pressure, and the world feels like it's falling apart! It's fair to say we're still not doing enough as a society to support young families and people of all backgrounds during this season of life.

Can we dare to dream of a society that believes we don't have to wait until later in life before satisfaction, happiness and contentment are possible? Research has found that more than half of Australians (63 percent) are sceptical on the basis they believe the government is only focused on short-term gains, not long-term challenges.[46] We've got to look after ourselves because others won't, or at least that's the narrative.

In the chapters to come, we're going to dive headlong into these issues. Not with blind optimism, but real strategies that will help you regain control of the stories you're telling yourself – the way you interpret and give meaning to all these stresses.

The good news is you can utilise the Story Code *regardless* of what's going on around you. It's a different way of processing world events, life events and the internal stories that run around in your head. It's the most exciting, challenging and inspiring idea I've worked on in years – and equally daunting. But you owe it to yourself and your loved ones to master the Story Code, rewrite your story and unlock your true potential. There's too much good work to be done in the world, and so many pitfalls to avoid.

Dr Renu Burr, an expert in leadership, business and coaching, told me we need to remove these internal obstacles because they can act as 'brakes' that slow us down and obscure our inherent capabilities. She added, "How do we remove the veils that hide our true essence and our true potential? We already have everything we need – it's there. And then we get in our own way."

So we get to the starting point. A decision to rewrite your story and overcome the lies, limiting beliefs and negative personal narratives holding you back. This is an invitation to become more self-aware and courageous.

To quote Sherilyn Shackell, founder and CEO of the Marketing Academy, speaking on my podcast:

> I believe that if people were really truly aware
> of what they were capable of achieving, every-
> body would sign up to as much development,
> inspiration, empowerment opportunities as
> they could find.[47]

I couldn't agree more.

CHAPTER 3

DECIPHER THE STORY CODE

"Transformation begins when you can start contextualising your story, struggles and self-doubts."

The Story Code is an idea I developed over several years on my journey of recovery. Working with health professionals, fitness coaches and spending time with mentors, it dawned on me that some of the storytelling techniques I'd developed for telling stories to external audiences apply equally to internal stories, the stories we tell ourselves.

On reflection, I was using a pattern I'd seen in business many times over. You'll often see marketplace competitors all heading in one direction, then out of the blue one of them will flip the script on a countervailing trend. For example, in 2025, Apple published a study that challenged a dominant AI narrative that caught my attention. It studied many of the popular LLMs (large language models) and generative AI platforms and ran them through a series of tests to examine their 'intelligence'. The result? Most of the AI systems failed.[1] Were these mysterious black boxes intelligent, or just great at high-speed pattern recognition? Putting details aside, it's a classic move – zig left when everyone's zagging right, and you'll stand out.

I remember the moment the seeds of *The Story Code* were formed. While speaking to a corporate audience about media and publishing, I explained my theory of magazine covers. Magazine publishers and editors aren't just great storytellers. They're experts at *knowing their audiences*. They conduct reader surveys, study which publications sell, or don't sell, and why. They speak with friends, colleagues and readers themselves about their story ideas to test and learn. It's both creative and strategic.

I've edited a few magazines in my career, and I loved this process of discovering what made audiences tick. There's a lot that business leaders, marketers and communications professionals can learn from the way journalists and editors connect the dots and weave together ideas that satisfy readers.

"Magazine covers are like a mirror," I said. "Readers need to see themselves reflected on the cover – if not directly, then at least as a projection of their future self. For example, *Bride to Be*. Do they put grooms on the cover? No. Not unless they want to go out of business. Lifestyle magazines don't publish pictures with serious business themes – they show mountains, bikes or people in active wear."

To apply the 'magazine as a mirror' metaphor, leaders need to look in the mirror to understand their own stories when faced with self-doubt, overwhelm and exhaustion. The mirror itself is a reflection that projects the opposite, or reversed image. So when we use the Story Code to rewrite the narrative, we're challenged to embrace the very opposite story we've been telling ourselves. A new preferred story begins to emerge from behind a dominant story of problems, suffering and inner turmoil. It's easy to fall into the trap of believing the problem story told by our inner critic: *I failed at that task, so I myself am a failure.* But what if the exact opposite were true? *It turns out, I am successful.*

What I discovered on my journey, and what I've seen in the lives of many leaders, is we've not yet assembled enough readily accessible evidence to remind ourselves in real-time that failure is part of the journey. We easily forget the many, many, many times when we've been successful on our own terms. That's the preferred story – the true reflection of who you are – that you need to remember.

CRYPTOLOGY OF STORYTELLING AND REWRITING THE NARRATIVE

When we dive into the body of academic research, it reflects, supports and extends the mirror metaphor in powerful ways. Essentially, if you want to break free from self-doubt and the destructive impact of telling yourself negative stories, studies consistently point to the value of unlocking personal stories that lift you up instead of holding you back.[2] The Story Code makes this process easy and accessible by helping you unlock the *right stories*. It's a relatively simple theory of change: create a pathway to health, healing and wellbeing by writing a new personal narrative that defines who you are and what you're becoming. The challenge, naturally enough, is that actually making this change in your life is quite a different story.

I was exploring this idea with Mark Yettica-Paulson. He works to bridge the communications divide between organisations and Indigenous communities. The Western mindset – particularly in business – doesn't typically warm to the idea that we need to explore our suffering and inner hardships by diving headfirst into a space where vulnerable, creative thinking is required. Personal transformation isn't for the faint-hearted.

Here's Mark's truth bomb:

> Part of the challenge with us making the changes we need to make is we're asking people to enter into a faith crisis willingly.
>
> The notion that you would question, "Wait a minute, so everything I believed in, I need to rethink this?" You can become stronger at the other side, or you can become more lost on the other side. And so to willingly ask people to enter into a faith crisis in order to find a new way is an everlasting challenge.

It's not necessarily a faith crisis in the sense of religion. Rather, it's the underlying belief systems that guide your life. Letting go is hard, particularly if there's a risk you could be worse off in terms of understanding what you really believe. However, even this perspective is just a story we tell ourselves: *Challenging my own beliefs is too risky.*

The first counterargument to the risk-avoidance mindset is that almost every successful person you admire has rewritten their story at some point in their lives. Dr Renu Burr arrived in Australia from India as a 20-year-old, only to discover her university studies in psychology weren't recognised. She was in the top ten in her course, but it didn't matter. So she started from the bottom.

Years later, she successfully battled cancer not once, but twice. She never changed her identity to that of a 'cancer survivor' – it was just an illness. "I just had to change my mindset. I changed my story of what was happening for me." If Renu can, so can you.

To further demonstrate the power of rewriting your story, let's look to seven-time world surfing champion Layne Beachley who discovered, at the age of 8, she was adopted. In her TEDx talk, she describes a deeply held limiting belief that she wasn't worthy of love. At the same time, she believed winning surfing contests would make the world love her.

Fast-forward to more recent times, and she's grown to embrace an entirely new narrative – one of love, wellbeing and encouraging others: "You can become a victim of your circumstances, or you become a master of your destiny. The choice is yours."[3]

The second counterargument to the risk-avoidance mindset is to remind you of my own story. There comes a point where sustained stress delivers you a biological response. It's much better to get help before you hit the proverbial tree, not afterwards, as my GP wisely told me.

So if you're in the grip of self-doubt in any shape or form, the invitation is – do something about it sooner rather than later! And as an extra bit of inspiration, all you need to get going is to start believing this journey is possible.

I love the growth mindset concept famously developed by Dr Carol Dweck. She teaches that leaders with a growth mindset believe in human potential and development, for themselves and others. They bring energy, excitement and possibility to the table. Dr Dweck wrote, "Instead of using the company as a vehicle for their greatness, they use it as an engine for growth – for themselves, the employees, and the company as a whole."[4]

Contrast that with a fixed mindset leader. These people care mostly about external validation. Change is resisted. They must always be right. It's a stifling environment, and honestly a miserable way to live.

Dr Dweck's TEDx talk summarises her approach nicely with the headline 'The Power of Yet'. For many of us, this journey begins with saying, "I've not rewritten my story *yet*."

STORY CODE IN-DEPTH DECIPHERMENT

Now let's do a deep dive into the Story Code to understand each segment and what it can unlock.

As a refresher, the four segments are:

- Challenge: Name the dragon – meet your inner critic

and uncover limiting beliefs.

- **O**verwrite: Reframe meaning – script your new lead character.
- **D**ecide: Make a decision – rewrite your story.
- **E**ncode: Develop healthy habits for life – change everything with your new story.

Using the Story Code to unlock your ideal life and story starts with taking the bold step of challenging the old narrative, including its biggest promotor: your inner critic.

Challenge: Name the Dragon – Meet Your Inner Critic and Uncover Limiting Beliefs

The inner critic is a source of negative opinion, one-liners and challenging statements that don't reflect the real you. You begin to master the Story Code by first becoming aware of and then challenging your inner critic. To borrow from mythology, it can help to think about it as the dragon – a strange and scary creature that flies in, causes chaos and flies off in a hurry.

From the very beginning, you start proactively framing the stories told by this detractive voice and symbolised by the dragon as part of your *old story*. The goal is to begin separating your identity or sense of self from the inner critic.

Using the Story Code to conquer your inner critic includes unlocking its kryptonite: your empowering *inner coach*. I'll confess I'm not a raging sports fan, but I've seen enough soccer coaches from the sidelines of my three sons' games to know a good one. Great coaches are inherently optimistic. They know which players are thriving and which ones are struggling. They see the whole game in all its glory and disappointment. And when the game is done, win or lose, they look to frame the experience in a way that's true, encouraging and practical. Next game, they might say, "We need to do a better job of calling for the ball," "Stay in your positions," "Pass quickly," and so on.

Thinking of the success-failure dynamic, what would your inner coach say? For example – yes, you missed the deadline today. Part of it was your fault because you started work on the task too late. But perhaps the scope of work was unrealistic, or you didn't have the necessary resources. Either way, it's not the end of the world – you'll get it done on time next week. Inner coach pops up: *Don't worry, you'll smash it next time. You've got a great track record!*

Where does your inner critic get its power and relevance? From your deeply held limiting beliefs. Limiting beliefs are the quiet rules we've internalised about what's possible for us. They operate in the background, shaping our decisions and reinforcing self-doubt.

A limiting belief is any assumption that shrinks your potential. It's the invisible script that tells you what you can and can't do, often without any real proof.

Limiting beliefs don't arrive overnight. They take shape over years – through childhood experiences, social conditioning, cultural messages, failures and even casual comments from others. But just because they've been around for a while, it doesn't mean they're accurate.

A limiting belief could sound something like, *I'm not good enough* or, *I don't have what it takes.* Essentially, limiting beliefs are stories you tell yourself about *who you are* – a bad leader, a subpar professional in your line of work, whatever the story is.

To move forward, we must take the radical assumption that the very opposite of those beliefs is true – or *will be true.*

Overwrite: Reframe Meaning – Script Your New Lead Character

The stories we tell ourselves can push us forward or hold us back. They define our character, for better or worse. They help us create meaning in the midst of life's circumstances. If we consider ourselves the lead character in the journey of life, using this segment of the Story Code, we can positively rescript that character if our inner critic and limiting beliefs – the dragon – have run riot.

In this segment, a key part of rewriting your story is identifying your Codebreaker Archetype – your true character, the
person you are or need to become. It doesn't matter if you're
not embodying all the characteristics right now because you
get to *overwrite* your current lead character with a new archetype. Your ideal self. The role you were born to play.

During the overwrite process, we'll dive deeper into the
seven Codebreaker Archetypes, which are:

- **The Hero:** Driven to undertake and accomplish
  bold missions
- **The Mentor:** Generous with and confident in
  own knowledge
- **The Navigator:** Organised, other-focused,
  driven to serve
- **The Futurist:** Hopeful, determined, goal-
  focused visionary
- **The Optimist:** Upbeat, leads with positive
  energy and fun
- **The Critic:** Quick to criticise and ask tough questions
- **The Phoenix:** Rises strong, reborn or transformed

Scripting your new lead character – the ideal, authentic,
wildly successful version of you – often means overwriting certain behaviours of your old character. I don't mean you need to
become a completely different person. Instead, the Story Code
helps you unlock the best version of you. The person you were

always meant to be. A lead character worthy of the new narrative you're about to write and, importantly, start living.

Decide: Make a Decision – Rewrite Your Story

Once you've reflected on your inner critic, limiting beliefs and archetype, a new narrative begins to emerge. The *decide* stage of the Story Code is where it all comes together. You're making a conscious decision to rewrite the narrative that defines you today and into the future. This is where real transformation occurs.

Your personal narrative is the overarching story you tell yourself about who you are, where you've been and where you're going. It shapes your identity, confidence and sense of purpose.

Leaning into the insights offered by the Codebreaker Archetypes, we can start to get context and clarity. Perhaps being the Hero in the 'hero's journey' seems to fit. Or maybe you're honest enough to face up to a darker version that haunts you – you've become the burnt-out Critic who's lost hope. Someone who revels in deep cynicism and a limiting belief that change is impossible for them, and the organisation.

If a bit of light comedy helps, I love a funny bit by *Flight of the Conchords,* "New Zealand's fourth most popular guitar-based digi-bongo acapella-gangsta-rap-funk-folk comedy duo." In a scene where they discuss a new stage musical with their manager, Murray, the boys reveal their inner critics:

Jemaine: "Our story is the story of two guys who start at the bottom, and with a lot of hard work continue along the bottom and finally end up at the bottom."

Murray: "Oh yeah, that's an intriguing scenario."

Bret: "Yeah, it's a rags-to-rags story."

Murray: "Imagine it. 'Yeah, did you see the one about the guys who started at the bottom, stayed at the bottom and at the end they were still at the bottom?'"

Bret: "Ah, yes, that's our lives."

Murray: "So inspirational! Who'd go and see that?"

Jemaine: "I think I'd see that."

Bret: "I would go and see that, yes."

Jemaine: "It's more realistic."[5]

Just brilliant.

If you were to use the Story Code to rewrite this narrative, the question you'd dare to ask is: What does the opposite of 'rags' look like for you? Do you dream about success in financial, relational, physical or emotional terms? What happens when you step into that mindset for just a moment? How far away does it feel?

Interrogating your personal narrative is a fascinating process. You might be happy enough with how things are for the moment – you're on a recovery trajectory like me, perhaps. The key to moving forward, however, is picturing your future self. This projection into the future is the ultimate expression of hope and courage. You're daring to picture yourself beyond a place where the walls seem to be closing in.

My future self, for example, is encouraging leaders all around the world to be their best selves, using the Story Code to rewrite their stories. My future self is someone who's content with who he is, regardless of external validation, and yet is energised by the knowledge he's helping leaders transform their lives at work – and beyond.

The decide segment of the Story Code is where all our intersecting ideas gather to paint a new, exciting picture of the road ahead:

- How your inner coach will behave in moments of trial, stress and suffering
- Healthy beliefs that inspire and motivate you
- A 'future self' who's compelling, exciting and a little bit terrifying!

Rewriting your story lets you express where you've been, where you are and where you're going. It brings together stories, feelings and dreams. Refined and edited over time, it's not perfect, but that doesn't matter. It's written primarily for an audience of one. And critically, there's no one right way of doing this, just as there's no right story that should define how you view success. For some, that will be freeing. For others, perhaps a little restrictive.

Here's a short version of my future story.

I'm a storyteller, a visionary and someone who loves connecting the dots between ideas. At my best, I've got energy and optimism to burn. I love encouraging leaders.

My inner coach is like an old friend who knows me well and nods quietly, "Hey, nice work. Keep it up!"

I've accepted that life isn't one continuous journey upwards. It's messier than I ever imagined, but that doesn't mean I need to stop moving forward or neglect recovering my strength.

I'm excited about encouraging leaders on their journeys because change is possible. Rewriting my story has made me a better man, a better husband, father and friend.

When life's tough, I choose to remember the good things. My successes at work, in relationships and with family – you know what they are, Mark! I'm already making a difference, and there's more to come.

Onwards.

A couple of things. Yes, it's weird to write something like that, and even more confronting to publish it in print. But at the same time, it's pretty cool. Reading that out loud feels great. It's who I am and how I'm approaching life right now. Compare that energy to those few years when I was a mess. There's no chance I could've reflected that level of clarity and confidence.

It's an encouraging perspective because I'm starting to find, as more people become aware of the Story Code, leaders are discovering how it can unlock different levels of personal transformation. One person told me she was "happy for the first time in a long time!" Her participation in my 'Flip the Script' coaching program was just one part of her story, but it's satisfying to hear how sustained focus and writing a new story is paying dividends. Another participant said the program arrived "at just the right time when it was time to change my story" and used it to take control of her life story. Isn't that the stuff of life?

Dr Renu Burr has a great way of explaining what's going on here. We move from telling our stories to living our stories. She explained, "So for me, it's very much about how do I listen to my story that I'm telling myself? Is it really true? That openness for me is really important." Many leaders lack self-compassion, she added. "We're hard on ourselves. If we don't shift our level of consciousness, we're going to get what we've always got. So it's either you take the challenge to look at a different way of seeing, being and doing, because we're not going to get there otherwise."

That level of consciousness is exactly what the Story Code unlocks.

Encode: Develop Healthy Habits for Life – Change Everything with Your New Story

The final stage of the Story Code, *encode*, is where transformation becomes sustainable. It's one thing to write a new story – it's another to live it every day, supported by small, healthy habits that change everything over time.

Neuroscience and behavioural economics show that our brains are wired to repeat old patterns because they feel familiar and safe. That's why even the most powerful insights can fade if they aren't reinforced.

Encode is about embedding your new story into small, repeatable habits that make your inner coach louder than your inner critic.

Now that we've deciphered the Story Code, it's time to do a deep dive into each segment and put it all into action. Let's get on with it, or 'lock in', as my kids would say.

CHALLENGE – MEET YOUR INNER CRITIC

(PART ONE)

FROM INNER CRITIC TO INNER COACH

"The stories you tell yourself today shape the person you'll become tomorrow."

*W*hat's the point of it all?

Walking up from Sydney's Wynyard Station towards my psychologist's office, I was in a very dark, moody place. It was midmorning; the sun was shining, and office workers were bustling around as usual – hunting for coffee, heading off to a meeting and spontaneously mingling on street corners with colleagues. I was trudging along, weaving between people, annoyed that I had to move out of their way.

Seriously, is there any point … to anything?

This was the voice of my *inner critic*, almost shouting inside my head as I scanned my surroundings, ears blocked from noisy chaos thanks to noise-cancelling headphones. Blocking out excessive noise had become essential in the aftermath of 2019's panic attack. My poor family was keenly aware of what stressed me out: chewing, loud bangs, doors, the dogs, four children doing normal kid things like being *loud*. Truthfully, I wasn't a great person to be around. I felt trapped. Stuck in a loop. The future was bleak. Looking back, it was textbook depression, stress and anxiety. A dark grey fog that followed me around, to my dismay.

At first, I didn't understand I had an inner critic. A lifelong optimist, I rarely dipped into negative thought patterns, and if I did, it was normally because I was hangry. The scary thing was, on a random street in the middle of Sydney, I had begun to believe my inner critic.

You work, you die.

It's the stuff of music, poetry, books and movies – plus I'd wrapped in a healthy dose of introspection.

Where did all these negative thoughts come from? Am I broken? Is this what happens when people go crazy and get locked up?

Then there was the shame injected into this journey from my faith life. Growing up in the church, I'd heard more than once the call to have faith and be strong and courageous. Bible verses like this really sting when you're depressed: "Rejoice in the Lord always; again, I will say rejoice!"[1]

Well, I'm not okay. So my faith is probably broken too.

It was honestly a shocking state of being. I could scarcely believe I was this depressed. So many negative voices were running through my head – it was almost too much. But whatever *this voice* was, I didn't want it.

The streets of Sydney faded away as I arrived at my psychologist's office. I'll call him Tim.

Exhausted, I sat down, and he handed me an assessment form called DASS-21 – the Depression, Anxiety and Stress Scale widely used by therapists and medical professionals. It was time for me to deliver another score so Tim could get a sense of how I was going.

The DASS-21 assessment contains 21 statements, and you rate each statement (0 to 3) according to how much it applies to you over the past week – in essence, a scale from 'never' to 'almost always'.

My experience of trudging up the street still fresh in my

mind, I stopped at statement 21: *I felt that life was meaningless.* The words jumped off the page. "Well, that's a solid three," I muttered. "Can I write four?"

Then the tears started flowing.

Here was a grown man in his mid-40s, once optimistic, completely bewildered by the negative voices in his head. An inner critic he'd never had, didn't understand and certainly didn't want.

WHAT IS AN INNER CRITIC?

Psychologists, therapists and experts call the inner critic a form of self-criticism, negative self-talk and cognitive distortion. Think about it as an annoying colleague who pops their head around the door at work, moments after you've been given a challenging new assignment, and says: "You're gonna fail at this. You're not even a real leader!"

The confronting thing is you probably already know exactly what I'm talking about. Most people experience the voice of their inner critic. It's always there, hiding away and taking notes as you go about your business. Keeping tabs on your greatest failures, embarrassments and moments of shame. That time you froze in a meeting and looked like an idiot? *Got it.* That questionable joke at family dinner? *Yep, in the memory and ready to play again at a moment's notice.* The time you turned up late for a business meeting, to your great embarrassment and shame. *Most definitely queued up for repeat.*

In her book *Thrive*, Arianna Huffington calls her inner critic an "obnoxious roommate."[2] That checks out. Not only does it say nasty things, but it causes you to think you're losing your mind. This was all a new experience for me and not part of any future I'd imagined.

It's only in recent times I've given my old inner critic a name – retrospectively if you like. Her name is 'Margaret', comedically named after the biting satire and humour of ABC's Margaret Pomeranz, famous for *At the Movies* and her segments on *The Weekly with Charlie Pickering*. Her savagely funny review of ABC's iconic children's show *Play School* stands out. In a deadpan voice, she describes how the soft toy character Humpty (Dumpty) was embraced by kids "despite debilitating vertigo."[3] Classic stuff!

Of course, all this isn't to say the real Margaret is a mean person. Over time, without too much conscious effort on my part, leaning into Margaret's persona helped me flip the script on my inner critic, compelling it to tell a new story.

Comedy is a great way to disarm an inner critic and lift you out of a rut.

WHERE DOES THE INNER VOICE COME FROM?

Neuroscience says our brains have evolved to prioritise threats for survival. Somewhere along the way, our inner critic decided that emotional threats – like rejection or failure – deserved the same alarm bells (triggered by the amygdala in the brain) as a charging predator. Handy in the wild, not so much in the office. And certainly not helpful if you're dealing with self-doubt, impostor phenomenon, anxiety and depression.

Psychologists Hal and Sidra Stone, creators of the Voice Dialogue process used in therapy, say the inner critic is a sub-personality that developed to protect people from shame and hurt.[4] It helps us defend ourselves against the trials and pressures of the world, and as we enter adulthood, it becomes a source of self-blame and negative self-talk.

Then we've got Sigmund Freud, who's a bit weird because of all that mother stuff, but his influence lingers. His version of the inner critic is the 'superego' – a type of internal moral authority. It guides behaviour by imposing and reinforcing moral standards. He also blames our parents for this superego because we learnt to admire and fear them while growing up. Apparently, as adults, we adopt their 'higher natures', which I think is code for growing to become like your mother or father.[5] I'm not sure how true that is for everyone, but what strikes me is the connection between Freud's idea and the way we think about parenting and our inner voice.

Psychologist Lev Vygotsky was one of the first to talk about how our voice as parents becomes our kids' inner voice. He says the words, and presumably tone, we use when speaking to our children or those in our care ultimately become their 'inner speech'.[6]

Gulp. I hope they remember all the good bits!

The good news is there's hope. In the pages to come, we'll discuss simple strategies to conquer your inner critic.

AWARENESS IS THE FIRST STEP TO TAMING THE INNER CRITIC

It might feel a bit morbid, but job number one on this journey is raising awareness and getting clarity – it's hard to rewrite your story if you don't know how truly bad the current story is in the first place.

Sometimes we know instinctively what the inner critic is saying. Other times it helps to have a guide. Here's a prompt we use to tackle it in workshops:

Q: What does your inner critic say about these aspects of your life?

Your Story	Inner Critic's Talk Track
My ambitions	
My value at work	
My beliefs	
My achievements	
My health	
My faith or spiritual life	
My lifestyle	

Did you identify any areas where your inner critic is controlling the narrative? Let's now take a look at some examples of stories your inner critic might be telling you.

To get us going, here's what Margaret has told me over the years.

- *I'm not a real journalist.*
- *I'm not a real CEO.*
- *I'm not smart enough to make a real difference in the world.*

Brutal, hey?

Ready for some more? These inner critic examples are what people have shared with me in workshops and private conversations.

- "I'm not smart."
- "I'll never succeed."
- "I'm not good enough."
- "I always get it wrong."
- "No one likes me."
- "I can't do anything right."
- "I'm a failure."
- "I'll never be as good as that person."
- "Why do I even bother?"
- "I can't stop now – work is my identity."

James Bond actor Daniel Craig has a great one he revealed on the *SmartLess* podcast: "I'm making this up as I go along."[7] Well, here's a newsflash – *we're all making stuff up*. That's how life works. We even celebrate this idea in Aussie culture. It's called 'giving it a crack'. Words can mean different things. It's your choice.

Author Ellen Hendriksen talks about the reality of making stuff up. "In truth, you gain confidence by doing things before you're ready."[8]

It's an echo of great parenting advice I picked up years ago. All first-time parents are worried they're not ready, but "when the baby is born, you're ready!" So, get on with it.

WHICH INNER CRITIC LINES HIT HOME?

Take a moment to go back and scan your inner critic's talk track. Which lines really hit home? Which ones are holding you back and impacting your life? If you're a scribbler, circle them right here in the book. And stay with me, because we're going to get stuck into some positive ways forward.

TURNING DOWN THE VOLUME

Turns out our inner voice can be really noisy. How do we turn down the volume over time? Can you really tune out these lies about who you really are?

Getting some time out in a quiet place isn't a bad idea, but that can be hard to achieve in a busy world. You need a sustainable way forward when your inner critic pops their head around the corner during a busy day of work.

The first step is to recognise the inner critic's voice for what it is: a story, not a fact. A lie or distortion of the truth. This is a critical point.

Late Australian psychologist Michael White, who together with New Zealander David Epston pioneered the development of narrative therapy, has a lot to say about how we explore the possibilities. Narrative therapy itself is one of the less recognised forms of therapy for patients and practitioners, but it's valuable for people looking for options outside of traditional cognitive processing or 'talk therapy' modes. The key to understanding the core of narrative therapy is identifying the problem, or stresses, that are causing issues.

For most of us, we're tempted to connect our problems with our identity. If we're not doing well, or even failing at something, it follows that we start thinking, *I'm a failure. Maybe I'm the problem. I'm not good enough.* Our inner voice is great at stirring up ideas like this.

The genius of narrative therapy comes when we begin to decouple negative self-talk from our sense of self. Problems, stresses and peaky moments in life when your inner critic's voice is loud – they're experiences, not who you are. I like the way White describes the narrative therapy approach:

"The problem becomes the problem, not the person."[9]

In other words, the problem you're dealing with at a moment in time no longer becomes the 'truth' about who you are. It doesn't mean we're not responsible for taking action or owning the consequences of our decisions. But it does give us a greater sense of agency to work on solutions – either on our own, with friends or with a qualified therapist or psychologist. The benefits? Researchers say a positive internal narrative directly impacts self-worth and addresses the impacts of impostor phenomenon.[10]

And it gets better. I spoke with David Newman, a narrative therapist at the Dulwich Centre (founded by Michael and Cheryl White) who explained a powerful philosophical and ethical underpinning of narrative practice. Every person is the expert in their own lives, people, families and communities. When their own insider knowledge is honoured, their lived experience is also honoured. They're not receiving intervention from a therapist; rather, they're positioned as a consultant who brings worthy knowledge to the conversation.

In the spirit of discovering how to master the Story Code, it's an exciting idea because traditional therapies, particularly talk-based approaches, tend to rob people of their own know-how, Newman told me, explaining:

We've got to develop practices whereby we can
assist people and families and communities to
recognise their know-how, especially when people
we meet have no sense of their worth. Maybe
they've been really beaten down by racism, poverty, homophobia or misogyny and have no sense
of their worth. We've got to develop practices
that assist people to have a sense that they have
worthy knowledge.

CONNECTING BUSINESS THREADS

Think about the connecting ideas for a moment. People are
experts in their own stories. They're not their problems. And
we can start objectifying these problems as stories with layers
that can be understood and explored through the lens of storytelling without destroying self-worth.

These ideas resonate deeply with me, and perhaps you, because we've seen this before in business, right? In leadership
environments, we learn to separate an organisation's value and
identity from the stresses and strains that shape their progress.
Poor client or customer experiences don't necessarily mean the
core identity of your organisation is broken. They're just problems that need fixing, regardless of how emotional you may
feel about them as a leader.

In fact, there's a great approach I picked up from a business methodology called the Entrepreneurs Operating System (EOS), which we use at ImpactInstitute.[11] It literally transformed my problem-solving mindset. EOS teaches you to effectively banish the word 'problem' and replace it with a less emotional word: 'issue'. Simplistically, collaborating on an issue is less emotive than working on a problem that carries all sorts of mysteries and long-lasting overtones.

Thankfully, there's more to it than playing around with words. Leadership teams working on an issue are taught to use a problem-solving tool called IDS – Identify, Discuss and Solve. First, in a team meeting, *identify* what is the real issue. Clarify who's raising the issue, what this person thinks the core issue is, and why it matters to the organisation. Next, the team *discusses* the issue – what's beneath the surface? How did the issue arise? What are all the interconnecting factors and implications? Finally, *solve*. Someone takes responsibility for a set of actions the team agrees is the best course of action, which is documented and reviewed during the next meeting.[12]

It's a delightfully pragmatic, logical and unemotional approach to problem-solving for hard-headed business types. And equally can feel a bit restrictive for other leaders who prefer a freewheeling, creative approach.

Regardless, the organisation's identity, and that of the leaders, are neatly separated from the issue at hand. IDS has worked a charm at ImpactInstitute, and likewise its echo in narrative therapy points to its value in our personal lives.

STARING AT THE CEILING

My only regret is I didn't discover the power of this approach in my own mental wellbeing journey much earlier.

A few days after that fateful day in Bunnings when my world fell apart, I found myself at Mum and Dad's house. Heather said I should take time out at their place while she kept the home fires burning – four kids and two dogs, plus her own consulting practice. It was a big, kind, generous offer.

And so, here I was, lying on my parents' spare bed staring blankly at the ceiling – and it wasn't even an interesting ceiling! *Margaret* was having a field day because here I was, back at home with my parents: *Well, you've really screwed this up now. You're back where you started. You're hopeless.* I remember feeling terrified. My identity and true sense of self felt like they were crumbling without my consent. I've always been a positive, energetic bloke. But now the fear of bad things to come descended like a fog, and I'd never felt less significant. Above me was this white ceiling. A giant mirror of nothingness that seemed to scream at me – "You've got nothing!"

Sadly, I've since learnt my experience is way more common than I'd ever dared to imagine, particularly for men like me in middle age. Mental health disorders such as depression, suicidality and loneliness are experienced by 1 in 4 Australian men during their lifetimes.[13] That's millions of men doing it tough daily, with an average of six men, and two women, ending their lives every day. *Nine people every single day.*[14]

Plenty of organisations are, of course, working on this issue, whether it's the Black Dog Institute, Lifeline or one of my favourites, Gotcha4Life, which is on a bold mission to end suicide. I learnt from Gotcha4Life's CEO, Belinda Elworthy, that despite all the work we've done in this space, there's still a perception among men, in particular, that sharing how we're feeling, or crying, is a sign of weakness. And regardless, no one wants to hear about your problems. Real men carry their own burdens.

That's not a newsflash, but it is remarkable how long it takes us to get help when we're struggling with our mental health – an average of 12 years. Twelve years![15] Belinda told me, "We've got to flip that script from, 'How do we solve this crisis?' to, 'How do we build a society that knows how to thrive despite the adversity that we all face?'"

INNER CRITIC'S EXISTENTIAL PROBLEM

We've been discussing the influence of your inner critic and separating your identity from 'the problem' so you can begin to address the issues holding you back. White and Epston's argument is this process of externalisation, and it's one of the first steps we can take. It's a process that opens up possibilities for people to describe themselves, situations and relationships in new ways.[16] People start taking a lighter, more effective and less stressed approach to 'deadly serious' problems. The trick, of course, is getting your head around the idea that the inner critic – a product of your own mind and experiences – isn't actually you. Or at least, it doesn't represent who you really are at your core. Mind games, anyone?

Well, from experience, the starting point on this journey is pushing through the awkward barrier. *Of course* it's weird to give your inner critic a name. *Of course* it's a bizarre idea to decide your inner critic's comments aren't part of who you really are. But the good news is, once you embrace these strange notions, you can move on, giving yourself a 'pat on the back' or allowing yourself to feel smug for just a moment – because pushing through means you're making progress. You've started working on the things holding you back or pulling you down.

HOW DOES IT SOUND?

Sound good? Great – but we're not done yet. There's plenty more to think about before we close out this chapter on the inner critic. That's because our inner critic is relentless and doesn't go away easily.

> **Just because you've decided to think about your issues in depersonalised, less emotional ways, it doesn't mean you're suddenly skipping down the street singing 'Happy' by Pharrell Williams.**

No, you've got to properly understand your inner critic to disarm its impact over time. And that means diving into something people with marketing backgrounds like me quite enjoy – figuring out its persona. That is, how does it sound? What does it look like, or who does it remind you of?

Remember my inner critic, Margaret? She's wry, cutting and sharp. Super confident and assertive in her opinion. I've had times in life when she's been quite convinced I won't succeed, like a cynical boss who's very hard to impress.

What about you? How would you describe your inner critic? You could borrow Margaret, but perhaps there's another character that comes to mind who deserves your comedic and therapeutic attention.

USE THE STORY CODE TO UNLOCK YOUR INNER COACH

Once you've thought about your inner critic, its name, and you've got a sense of how it thinks and feels, it's time to use the Story Code to unlock your inner coach.

Think about a story or one-liner you frequently hear from your inner critic. To use one of my earlier examples: *I'm not actually that smart.* The breakthrough comes when you dare to believe the exact opposite of this line, transforming your inner critic into your inner coach: *Hey, it turns out I'm pretty smart after all!*

It's a real example for me too. A decade ago, I was being coached by one of Australia's leading futurists and keynote speakers. Reflecting on my personality with a throwaway line, he said, "Smart guys like you."

At the time, my inner critic, Margaret, was dialled in. *No I'm not!* she snapped instantly. These days, I've dialled down Margaret and replaced her with an inner coach, who I'll confess I've not named, largely because it just feels like me.

The point is, over the past few years, I've been using the Story Code to remember moments in time when the evidence showed I was, in fact, reasonably smart! Not Einstein clever, but good enough. The right mix of applied experience, wisdom and in-the-moment smarts that helped me make good decisions and respond to situations at home and work in useful ways.

For example – and forgive the lack of modesty – my first book *Beliefonomics* had at least one clever idea that impressed readers. I discovered this when one of my agency partners, a man who runs one of the largest creative agencies in Sweden, told me he was professionally jealous! It was the first time in his career he'd seen a storytelling framework that combined customer psychographics, brand journeys and marketing channels. For context, in the 2 years leading up to the book's release, I wasn't 100 percent confident I had something unique or super smart. So my client's vote of confidence that sunny day outside a coffee shop in Stockholm made my day.

Now it's time to fully unlock your inner coach by countering each negative story your inner critic spouts with a flipped positive version. For example, *I can't do that, I'm not smart enough* (inner critic) becomes, *I can do that, I've got what it takes* (inner coach).

Inner Critic Categories	Inner Critic's Talk Track	Inner Coach
My ambitions		
My value at work		
My beliefs		
My achievements		
My health		
My faith or spiritual life		
My lifestyle		

LET YOUR INNER COACH CONTROL THE NARRATIVE

Now, what strikes me is how it doesn't take much to flick back to that moment in my mind's eye when Margaret steps out of the shadows and challenges my intelligence or confidence. It's just a decision to remember the evidence, or examples, that prove Margaret wrong.

And that's the power of using the Story Code to unlock your inner coach and put your inner critic back in their place. The simple fact is you and I are not easily fooled! We *know* when we're lying to ourselves. That has always been the big problem I've had with peppy self-talk and trite inspirational statements.

The world isn't all sunshine and rainbows. It doesn't always have a happy ending for every person, and all the car stickers in the world can't change that!

So what *is* true? What *is* effective? Examples in your own life where you know you have, in fact, succeeded. You did a great job. You were brave when you didn't think you had it in you.

When working to keep the inner coach in control of the narrative, it can help to complete a simple to–from dichotomy table.

Ask yourself, how would you summarise this journey *from* an inner critic *to* an inner coach? Here's an example, but feel free to create your own table with relevant keywords.

110

My Commitment to Change

From		To
From		**To**
Hopeless	➡	Hopeful
Anxious	➡	Confident
Self-doubting	➡	Courageous
Burnt out	➡	Energised
Defeated	➡	Ambitious
Pessimistic	➡	Optimistic
Surviving	➡	Thriving

At this stage of the journey, the challenge you're facing is daring to spend more time deliberately remembering great stories in your life so you can quickly drown out your inner critic.

THINK BACK AND HAVE A CRACK

Take a moment right now to jot down a great story from your life where you were quite smart, bold, courageous or funny.

The key is to think of a story that seems to challenge the most common story your inner critic tells you. In other words, whatever feels like the most unbelievable example of you actually doing well, succeeding or overcoming your fears. The fun thing that might happen, which happened for me, is once you start going back in your mental database, you suddenly find more great examples.

In my case, I interviewed a CEO for my podcast, and he mentioned being happy to speak with me because I was "smart" and our conversations over the years were always interesting. Ain't that nice? It was super satisfying because my inner coach has been training me to keep an ear out for affirming statements that shut down Margaret.

Ultimately, your inner coach should have the loudest voice.

CHALLENGE – MEET YOUR INNER CRITIC
(PART TWO)

FROM LIMITING BELIEFS TO HEALTHY BELIEFS

"Everyone lies to
themselves in a crisis
because we're too close
to our own story."

Meet inner critic's partner in emotional and psychological harm, *limiting beliefs*. Think of them as lies or false beliefs we hold about ourselves. They keep us from chasing goals and dreams, and pursuing relationships, and they form mental boundaries that direct our behaviour. When left unchecked, they can become a core part of our character.

Mark Manson writes about three flavours of limiting beliefs:

1. Limiting beliefs about *yourself* – something is wrong with you.
2. Limiting beliefs about the *world* – people won't let you do things.
3. Limiting beliefs about *life* – you can't do something because it's too hard.[1]

The key consideration across all aspects of work and personal life is: these limiting beliefs hold you back. They're directly responsible for making you feel stuck, unable to move forward or unable to do exciting things in the future. They're almost like an immovable wall in your mind. Sometimes conscious, other times subconsciously acting to influence your decisions.

Here are some classic examples:

- "I don't have what it takes to really succeed."
- "Others are more talented and better than me."
- "I won't get that promotion until I'm perfect at this role."

The insidious thing about limiting beliefs like these is they're not always top of mind. Instead, they're hiding somewhere in your sub-consciousness.

Limiting beliefs are deep-seated beliefs or worldviews that set us up for disappointment and failure. They shape your identity, your capability, and your hope for the future – or lack of it.

Here's a confronting example from my own journey: I used to doubt I could really succeed in business. This limiting belief hung around for years despite the objective fact that my wife and I co-founded Filtered Media 15 years ago. We successfully sailed past the infamous '7-year itch' when many small businesses fail. This business supported us while we raised our four kids. And today it lives on in the form of two entities that merged to become ImpactInstitute. Remarkably, the merger was successful. Most mergers fail. To illustrate, on hearing the merger news, one of our clients wryly said to me, "We'll see how you go."

Now to be clear, I know it takes great leadership, but business isn't a solo sport. Our organisation is successful because we have an incredible team. For example, our Disability Expo events attract around 50,000 visitors and 1,500 exhibitors each year, giving people in the disability community and service providers a psychologically safe and practically useful environment in which to help one another. You don't bring over ten big expo events to life around Australia without a team of dedicated people who care about detail and are prepared to work. Meanwhile, our brand storytelling and impact advisory team has won awards, done incredible work and attracted loyal clients, some sticking with us for as long as a decade.

I tell you all this because, you know what? Back in 2005 when I was a journalist and editor, I secretly doubted I'd be very good in business. I didn't know if I had what it took to be a good leader. Why? Well, it's humbling to admit, but a survey told me so! A now extinct magazine called *Business Review Weekly* published an interactive survey on their website that gave me serious pause for thought. You answered a bunch of questions, and it spat out your results – *Do you have what it takes to be an entrepreneur?* My result: *Not yet!* It recommended I get more experience and have a bigger risk appetite. Yikes.

I sat at my desk and laughed it off while experiencing a quiet sinking feeling. I didn't realise it at the time, but this was the moment I started fostering a limiting belief: *I'm not ready to be an entrepreneur.* After all, my identity was wrapped up in being a journalist and editor. One of my favourite quips was: "Nothing about journalism teaches you how to run a business." It's not true, of course, but I started thinking that perhaps it might be.

CONTEXT IS EVERYTHING

So let's do a quick recap of my story. I started to develop a limiting belief around my future potential as a business leader and entrepreneur. I'd unwittingly scripted a character who was destined to fail. Looking back, I can see how my limiting belief fed my inner critic, Margaret. She was having a field day!

When our little agency business started in the late 2000s, she was always feeding my self-doubt. Things like: *That client hasn't called you back yet. They're probably going to sack you.* Now, the real reason was people are simply *busy.* They've got other things to do that are more important than calling me back within the hour! It was a tough lesson because I'd come off the back of being IT Editor at the *Australian Financial Review.* It's the kind of journalism gig where people call you back pretty quickly because they want to get quoted in the newspaper.

The trouble we all face in moments like this is we have a choice – foster the negative narrative or choose to tell ourselves a better story. Sounds Captain Obvious, doesn't it? Except that when you're in the thick of it – multitasking, trying to grow a new business and doing things you've never done before – it's very easy to lose perspective. And it's even easier to lose perspective when you're allowing your inner critic and limiting beliefs to run riot for days, weeks and months on end.

One of the catch-all labels we hear in psychology and

leadership describing scenarios like this is impostor syndrome, which I think is better named impostor phenomenon because it's not actually a disease or biological deficit.

> **You don't 'catch' impostor phenomenon one day like the common cold! It's a feeling that grows slowly over time, continuously fed by countless events and interactions at work each day.**

And so my early business years really did swing between moments of elation and outrageous confidence and bouts of impostor phenomenon – not that I told anyone. Thankfully, I learnt not to dismiss this emotional ride as youthful ignorance and inexperience, even though both also applied. The truth was, I'd started down an entrepreneurial career path with a secret set of limiting beliefs that held me back from completely embracing every opportunity and properly enjoying our success. Left alone, limiting beliefs and your inner critic can slowly become part of your identity, ingraining themselves in your character and making you feel captive to a destructive idea or a lie about your potential.

LIMITING BELIEFS UNPACKED

People often ask me for examples of limiting beliefs, so let's look at some fictional scenarios. I want to show you they can combine with your inner critic to really slow you down when you encounter very normal situational triggers.

Career and Success

Trigger: You hear about an exciting new job within your organisation.

Inner critic: *I'm not good enough to apply for that promotion yet. Probably need more experience.*

Underlying limiting belief: *People like me don't manage teams well.*

Relationships

Trigger: You get a short, harsh email from your manager or client.

Inner critic: *I've done it again. I keep misreading situations!*

Underlying limiting belief: *I didn't deserve this job in the first place.*

Professional Growth

Trigger: A meeting with your manager at the start of a new financial year. She asks what professional growth goals you'd like to set.

Inner critic: *No point setting goals if I'm gonna fail!*

Underlying limiting belief: *I'm bad at my job.*

Creativity and Innovation

Trigger: The team gathers for a brainstorming session because it needs new product ideas.

Inner critic: *I've got nothing to say.*

Underlying limiting belief: *I'm not creative. None of my ideas are good.*

Networking Events

Trigger: You walk into a large room for pre-dinner networking drinks at a gala awards night.

Inner critic: *I hate these moments – I'm no good at small talk.*

Underlying limiting belief: *Most people are more interesting than me.*

Health and Wellness

Trigger: Your boss casually talks about their new exercise regime that begins at 5 am every day.

Inner critic: *I could never do that – I'm too lazy!*

Underlying limiting belief: *I'll never be a fit, energetic person.*

How many of those situations ring true? Likely more than a few. The key is to pay attention to how your inner critic and your limiting beliefs are working arm in arm. They love feeding your self-doubt and revel in moments when impostor phenomenon takes over.

The good news? You can challenge any limiting beliefs and trade the inner critic for the inner coach.

USE THE STORY CODE TO CHALLENGE LIMITING BELIEFS

Now let's look at what can happen when we use the Story Code to rewrite these same scenarios. To deliberately explore the opposite perspective, you must approach the situation with a fresh mindset and a determination to change for the better. When your inner critic becomes your inner coach, you start fostering healthy, empowering beliefs. Negative becomes positive. Cynical becomes optimistic. Hopeless becomes hopeful.

Career and Success

Trigger: You hear about an exciting new job within your organisation.

Inner coach: *I'll throw my hat in the ring.*

Underlying healthy belief: *I'm sure I can figure out how to do that job.*

Relationships

Trigger: You get a short, harsh email from your manager.

Inner coach: *Don't take that personally. I better find out what's going on.*

Underlying healthy belief: *I know I'm doing well, but there are always opportunities to learn.*

Professional Growth

Trigger: A meeting with your manager at the start of a new financial year. She asks what professional growth goals you'd like to set.

Inner coach: *This is a great opportunity to keep growing.*

Underlying healthy belief: *A growth mindset will help me be successful in the long term.*

Creativity and Innovation

Trigger: The team gathers for a brainstorming session – we need new product ideas!

Inner coach: *Let's just give this a go. I might surprise myself.*

Underlying healthy belief: *Great things happen when teams gather.*

Networking Events

Trigger: You walk into a large room for pre-dinner networking drinks at a gala awards night.

Inner coach: *I wonder who's here? I'm curious to learn something new.*

Underlying healthy belief: *People always have interesting stories. I just have to ask!*

Health and Wellness

Trigger: Your boss casually talks about their new exercise regime that begins at 5 am every day.

Inner coach: *I wonder what I can learn about their approach.*

Underlying healthy belief: *There are lots of different ways to stay healthy.*

Quite the contrast, eh? Night and day. That said, you might be thinking, *Yeah, Mark, but it's not that easy. You can't just flip your thinking instantly.* Well, no, you're right. It's not easy. But it is achievable over time. It takes effort, focus, determination and other positive actions. The bottom line is you really can choose to rewrite the stories you tell yourself.

INTERROGATE YOUR LIMITING BELIEFS

We've now seen how limiting beliefs can hold us back and how empowering beliefs can open the way forward. But the question remains: How do we actually make the shift? One method I use is what I call the Mirror Mindset. Imagine holding up a mirror to your inner critic. Whatever story it tells you – you're not good enough; you'll never succeed; you don't belong here – the mirror flips it to its opposite. What if the opposite were true? This isn't wishful thinking; it's a disciplined practice of searching your own life for evidence that supports the mirrored version of your story. When you find it, you discover that the critic's voice isn't the only truth available. In fact, the mirror reveals a more empowering narrative you can choose to inhabit. Here's how.

First, list all the limiting beliefs that are holding you back, for example, *I'm not good enough* or, *Success doesn't come to people like me.*

Next, answer several key questions:

- When did I first start believing this line was true?
- What was the trigger? A person or event?
- How often do I tell myself this story?

Now comes the fun part where we use the Story Code and Mirror Mindset to rewrite those limiting beliefs. Ask yourself about the exact opposite idea. What's a positive version of each limiting belief you can integrate into your story? For example:

- *I'm a failure* becomes, *I'm successful.*
- *I don't have any skills* becomes, *I'm developing valuable skills.*
- *I don't have anything interesting to say* becomes, *My story is interesting – my experiences are valuable!*

Once you've identified some healthy beliefs, the next step is to start believing them.

POWER OF CULTIVATING
HEALTHY BELIEFS

Let's look more closely at healthy beliefs and how they can become a long-term foundation of your new narrative. Healthy beliefs do what it says on the tin. They're positive, hopeful, future-oriented convictions about how the world works.

I asked Sasha Titchkosky, co-founder and CEO at Koskela, an ethical B-Corp-certified design and furniture brand in Australia, about her healthy beliefs: "I believe in myself. I believe I can do it. And I surround myself with positivity." No fuss, no glamour. Just a commitment to moving forward in a leadership role that requires tenacity and a clear-eyed perspective on the future. Healthy beliefs are kept alive by choosing your colleagues, friends and community wisely. People who share your vision, values and sense of optimism.

In *Beliefonomics*, I talk about core beliefs like Titchkosky's as assumed truths that deeply impact our decisions and worldview. They shape everything from the clothes we wear to the products we buy:

> Our belief systems are collections of mythologies, stories and world views that fundamentally influence our behaviour. Our beliefs shape everything from the clothing on our backs and the words we use to the products we buy.

> Beliefs are the fuel for fires we see every day
> in the news across the spectrum of politics, re-
> ligion and government. Does truth matter? Do
> you believe in democracy? What about climate
> change – a scientific hoax? Our belief systems
> reach into every part of our lives and through
> storytelling are pivotal agents of change. In busi-
> ness, we ignore them at our peril.[2]

It's a perspective I formed during a 5-year journey exploring the heartbeat of storytelling. I wanted to know what, in essence, made stories work. Why are some stories so compelling and impactful that they change our lives? And why do others fall flat?

The business problem I was wrestling with was the fact customers are increasingly distrustful of brands. We're bombarded with too many messages, on too many platforms, and the signal-to-noise ratio is too heavy on the noise side. If you're a company trying to get its message out to the public or your niche set of customers, how can you tell the right story that will resonate and ultimately help you drive growth?

The answer, in part, is business leaders need to understand what their customers *believe*. What we believe about the world – across politics, religion and existential ideas – is the heartbeat of brilliant storytelling. Stories, or corporate narratives, resonate with us when they align with how we see the world. The same applies when we start thinking about the stories we tell ourselves.

Limiting beliefs are reinforced and fuelled by the stories from your inner critic, as we've seen in the previous examples. They're not interested in healthy, positive progress. They're inherently conservative, risk-averse and not interested in any newfangled ideas that make you uncomfortable.

In contrast, healthy beliefs are deliberately seasoned with optimism, hope and positive facts from your own lived experience. They inspire us to explore solutions, not give up, and ask more questions. We're not done, even when the situation looks overwhelming. They're the emotional, mental and spiritual foundations of our lives. They're key to unlocking the Story Code to consciously write our unfolding personal narratives.

We're choosing to rewrite the stories we tell ourselves by leaning on the insights gained from examining what we really believe about the world.

Hollywood screenwriter Robert McKee had this to say about storytelling and his own sense of meaning: "Human beings suffer. That's what it is to be alive, to suffer. Anything that a person can do to alleviate the suffering in others is a good thing, a positive thing, a meaningful thing. Stories do exactly that. They make life liveable."[3]

Story is a kind of balm that soothes the inevitable stresses, suffering and heartache we encounter at work and all aspects of life. And I'd go even further than McKee and say that stories are how we make life meaningful, not just liveable. Rewriting your story is effectively holding up a mirror to yourself and choosing to believe there's a better way than believing and repeating the stories that hold you down.

BUT ISN'T THIS ALL A BIT WEIRD?

Okay, now let's pause for a second. You might be thinking, *Isn't talking to ourselves, telling ourselves stories a bit weird? A bit woo-woo? I don't do woo-woo.* Well, I can't speak for everyone, including people who work with healthcare experts to address serious conditions such as schizophrenia, bipolar, or psychosis. But in general, talking to ourselves is a perfectly normal part of life. It begins when we're children and continues right throughout life, to a greater or lesser degree depending on the person. We speak to ourselves as a form of motivation, to help find things, stay focused, or process difficult moments.[4] How often have you seen sports people shout out loud to themselves, "You can do this!"?

The challenge for people experiencing self-doubt, burnout, stressful moments or the normal weariness of everyday working life is: the stories we tell ourselves can easily slide from positive to negative. We forget all the good stories in our lives. Our inner critic wears away at our sense of self, reinforcing limiting beliefs and creating a reinforced story loop. Instead of assuming the winning lead character role, we end up living as side characters in our own lives.

CRYPTOLOGY OF OUR BELIEF SYSTEMS

So how do we go about embracing a new set of healthy beliefs? Firstly, we must understand the cryptology of how our belief systems operate. That is, the hidden codes, patterns and rules that silently govern how our beliefs are formed, protected and sometimes encrypted against change – much like a cipher (or system for disguising information) that must be cracked before transformation is possible.

Dr Carol Dweck says the first step is to recognise that our beliefs aren't fixed in stone. They naturally evolve over time. In *Mindset: Changing the Way You Think to Fulfil Your Potential*, she writes about 1960s psychiatrist and cognitive therapy pioneer Aaron Beck who discovered that his clients' *beliefs* were at the heart of their problems. Beck was among the first to help clients discover and then change their beliefs in an intentional, positive way. Dr Dweck says whether we're aware of it or not, all people keep a running account of what's happening to them, what it means and what they should do in response – resist change, or embrace change. She calls it the choice between a fixed mindset and a growth mindset.[5]

Someone with a growth mindset is open to change. In effect, they say to themselves: *I can't do (that new thing) yet.* 'Yet' is the key word here. It's Dweck's gift to the world, if you will. It certainly changed my life when we first dug into the growth mindset thinking back in the 2010s during the early days of Filtered Media. Looking at this through the lens of my *Business Review Weekly* story, my limiting belief was I wasn't a 'real' entrepreneur. I didn't believe 'yet' would ever come.

Turns out the opposite was true. A few years ago, I took another online survey and discovered that my high tolerance for risk and my big-picture thinking were ideally suited to the entrepreneurial life! It gave me the evidence needed to rewrite my story, deliberately focusing on using Dweck's 'yet' mindset to foster a healthy belief – *I'm always growing and getting better.* It's a mindset that embraces learning and accepts failures or mistakes as a necessary part of the process. Instead of surrendering to self-doubt, healthy beliefs use the power of 'yet' as a call to positive action.

SCRIPT A NEW SET OF HEALTHY BELIEFS

Someone who embodies a growth mindset and actively embraces healthy beliefs is Daniel Davis, an expert EOS implementer and business advisor. Daniel has walked with me and the team for many years, and we wouldn't be where we are without his coaching and clear thinking.

What's remarkable about his story is the starting point. His dad left when he was born. Growing up in Western Sydney, Daniel had multiple stepfathers and attended 13 schools before he completed primary school. He was the only man in their family for two generations who hadn't been to jail. Unemployment was a big part of his family's story, and in his words, "There were a lot of assumed outcomes for a person who gets raised like that." Talk about an opportunity for devastating limiting beliefs to hijack your life story! It's easy to believe that anyone in that situation could think they're doomed to endure poverty, struggle and poor life outcomes.

The turning point in Daniel's life came at the young age of 10 when he got a job working at a timber yard in Regents Park (age wasn't a problem in the 1980s!). His story began to change thanks to the people he met in that timber yard – men who took him under their wing and literally transformed his future. Daniel explained:

> When I was at the workplace, I wasn't around schoolyard police. I wasn't around a negative family. I was around workmates, and these work-mates treated me very, very different, and they said, "Hey, you're doing a great job. Hey, geez, you're a hard worker." In other words, there's compliments coming my way for the first time in my life. Never had it before.

And I think that moment stands out as the point where I started to question the narrative that may have been in my head prior around *what are my limitations?* I started to look and think, maybe, maybe there's a chance here that life would be different.

I think the positivity of workmates and the small little chats that you'd have with people is what made me think, well, who knows what's possible?

Lots, as it turns out. By age 13, Daniel had three jobs, left home and was living on his own, paying rent and looking after himself (again, despite his age!). He went on to finish school and began working in service stations with a Lebanese family where he discovered a passion for small business. What followed was a remarkable series of events as his boss backed him to begin managing one service station, then three retail stores at age 21.

Newly married, Daniel then set his ambitions higher. With help from his employer and mentor, he bought an IGA store in Blackheath. Long story short, his experience in small business led to him bringing EOS to Australia – he was the first person to run the practice outside of North America, helping business owners streamline and scale their companies.

Success followed, with Daniel ultimately supporting 40

companies, completely fulfilling his potential as a business coach. Limiting beliefs utterly smashed.

Now, a quick postscript in Daniel's story is he did burn out at one point, prompting him to halve his client load and move out of the city for a slower, more sustainable lifestyle that restored a greater sense of wellbeing.

What stuck with me, and the lesson to share, is that not only is Daniel one of many Australians who rose above humble beginnings, but he embodies a growth mindset and our definition of healthy beliefs. For example, in one of our coaching sessions, Daniel challenged some of our team members who were uncomfortable moving from client delivery to sales roles – they confessed to knowing very little about sales. Daniel explained:

> I remember challenging everyone and saying,
> "What do you mean? What is sales exactly?" I
> said, "You're helping people. You're going out and
> helping people. You're not selling them something
> they don't want or need. You're helping people.
> That's what we do with this business. We shift our
> mindset to, *How can we help them?*

A limiting belief says, *I can't do sales.* A healthy belief says, *Sales is helping people with something they need.*

It's one thing to hear something like that from a random

business coach, and an entirely different thing to hear it from a man who has literally rewritten his story.

OPPORTUNITY COST – WHAT DO YOU HAVE TO LOSE?

As we start to wrap up this chapter, a word of warning. In business, leaders like to talk about opportunity cost. It's a fancy way of asking what will happen if we *don't* take action. What benefits, personal growth and new experiences will you miss out on if you don't move forward on this path from self-doubt to success on your terms? Well, let me spell out a few opportunity costs or negative outcomes from a career perspective:

- Your ability to realise goals, take advantage of new opportunities at work and help your organisation grow will be limited.
- You may not develop the resilience, adaptability and growth mindset needed to mature fully as a leader in the workplace and at home.
- Holding on to negative, destructive or unhelpful limiting beliefs could impact your physical, mental and spiritual wellbeing.

There are, of course, many, many ways of supporting your physical, mental and spiritual wellbeing. The stories you tell yourself don't live in isolation, and I don't for a second think of them as the metaphorical silver bullet. *Yet*, the pervasive, persistent and insidious nature of limiting beliefs should not be underestimated. From experience, I know they harden over time. Negative self-beliefs can, for some of us, become harder and harder to shift as we get older.

An interesting research paper by Australian psychologists Michael H Connors and Peter W Halligan explores the cryptology of our belief systems. The researchers make the case that beliefs are, generally speaking, difficult to change if they're well-formed over time. Confirmation bias seems to play a big part in our thinking. We resist new ideas that challenge existing beliefs. "People, for example, tend to seek confirmatory information that supports their belief and be overly influenced by the information."[6]

That's an idea you often hear people talk about regarding the state of the news media, for example. The United States, Australia and many Western nations are becoming increasingly polarised in left and right political and ideological tribes. People with progressive, liberal beliefs tend to gravitate towards certain media outlets, while others with more traditionally conservative or 'hard right' views find themselves spending more time with media attuned to this way of thinking. Without going too far down this rabbit hole, it's a great way of understanding our journey from self-doubt to success.

Limiting beliefs aren't just yours; they're shared by others.

We're all tribal. Most of us, myself included, profess to be open to and curious about the world around us. And yet we're so close to our own stories and so engaged in various tribes, like those facilitated by the media, that it takes proper effort to change. You have to *want* to change. I'm not here to make you. I gave up my ill-advised dreams of starting a cult years ago. Just kidding! But also, I'm serious. I'm so passionate about encouraging people to lean into new opportunities – because change is possible.

If you're ready, let's keep going because the next chapter will take you one step closer to practical, meaningful and exciting change.

OVERWRITE – SCRIPT YOUR NEW LEAD CHARACTER

"You're the master storyteller of your own life, so don't let anyone else write the script."

Brooke Shields grew up as a child actor and model. Famous for movies like *The Blue Lagoon, Pretty Baby* and *Mother of the Bride,* she's now a bit older. Nearly 60, in fact. She popped up on my radar recently when I came across an article about her new book, *Brooke Shields Is Not Allowed to Get Old: Thoughts on Ageing as a Woman.* What a great hook – she said the quiet bit out loud!

Society projects so many expectations at women. Look like *this,* act like *that.* To recap: here's a woman who's spent a lifetime under the media spotlight. We'd expect her to endure more scrutiny than most. Yet what's interesting about her approach is how openly, honestly and vulnerably she has put her experiences into print. It's obviously beyond my experience, but I've heard women talk about how they feel invisible when they get to a *certain age.* Shields flips the script by going large – making herself and her story visible. She's not going to stay in the shadows. She's not going to conform to your ideas about how women should behave as they get older. That's because she has come to terms with her inner critic and silenced the voices telling her how to live, and now she's out to change the narrative.

No doubt Shields's story is an inspiration for women around the world dealing with the stress, anxiety and suffering related to this issue. She said a survey of 2,000 women found they criticise themselves at least eight times per day, which she called a low number.[1] Her solution to this crisis at scale is – you guessed it – learning how to rewrite your story to embrace greater power and self-confidence. Now, that sentence probably sounds a bit self-helpy, but she's not taking herself too seriously:

> I'm finding a sense of humor about myself. And it's not just self-deprecation, which used to be my source of humor. Because here's the thing about putting yourself down all the time – even if it's in a jokey way: Eventually, you start to believe it to be true. And that's dangerous.[2]

What I love about this story is that with renewed confidence and clarity about her personal narrative – confronting prejudice – Shields now walks into rooms standing taller. That's a great definition of success right there.

Think about that scenario for a moment. It doesn't matter what you or I think about her, her journey or even her movies! What matters is she's now behaving in ways that are true to herself and her new personal narrative. She's quite *visible*. She's confident and knows she's bringing something unique to the world.

A few lessons to grab hold of here.

First, laughing really is great medicine. Don't stay so serious! I'm also speaking to myself here. Journeying out of the dark recesses of anxiety and depression, I discovered that comedians were a lifeline. I'd lost the ability to crack dad jokes and make people smile, but not the ability to find funny stuff to make *me* smile.

Second, Shields illustrates a type of storytelling archetype called the Mentor. Mentors are people who have recovered from trauma, hurt or difficult experiences and have valuable wisdom to share. They're generous and willing to share their expertise. Confident in their own knowledge and experience, they're on the lookout for opportunities to connect and invest in the right people who can benefit from their mentorship.

We see this archetype in all sorts of formats – documentaries, TV shows, movies and leadership profiles in business media. Confident leaders join others on a journey, offering their wisdom and expertise in appropriate settings. Executive coaching is, of course, where we see this most often in the workplace.

A movie that illustrates this well is *Karate Kid: Legends* (2025), part of a franchise reboot that stars Jackie Chan (Mr Han) and Ralph Macchio (Daniel LaRusso) as two mentors to a teenage kung fu prodigy, Li Fong (played by Ben Wang).[3] As we know from the first *Karate Kid* (1984), the hero of our story can't succeed without the help of a mentor – in that case, the iconic Mr Miyagi (Pat Morita).[4] All three mentors have core traits instantly recognisable: wise, calm, patient teachers, the right mix of tough love and compassion, and somewhat reluctant to step into the mentorship role – something we often see in modern leadership circles (false humility, perhaps?). Of course, mentors are never perfect, but they are essential if the hero is to succeed.

If we go back to Brooke Shields, she's clearly not a perfect mentor. Yet she has experienced real human discrimination and suffering and is determined to make an impact by telling her story. I've got no doubt she'd make an amazing mentor, and her book is a great step in that direction.

As we explore the role of storytelling archetypes, the key idea is they're *evocative* – that is, they resonate deeply with us in ways that aren't always immediately obvious. Let me explain.

Carl Jung says these archetypes live in our *collective consciousness*.[5] There are shared symbols and story patterns we absorb from a range of sources: art, religion, folklore, myths and, by my measure, the stories we see playing out on the national and global stages.

Then there's the moment Joseph Campbell calls "meeting with the mentor."[6] This could be a more experienced leader you meet in business who, instinctively, you know is someone you want to spend more time with. There's a sense they could be an important positive influence on your career. Guidance, wisdom and some kind of external recognition that we're on a shared journey are deeply human needs.

DISCOVER YOUR ARCHETYPE

I suspect that very few of us think about archetypes and how they might apply to our own lives. And yet that's what we're going to do here. Why? Because it's the key to mastering the Story Code and rewriting your story.

I've found that when people discover their personal archetype, it's transformational because leaders begin to understand themselves within the context of universal story patterns.

Campbell's great contribution to storytelling was the insight that myths tend to follow the same arc across time. That's not a bad thing, mind you. For someone who's feeling stuck, it unlocks a different perspective – regardless of how you feel today, you're still living within the context of a larger story that keeps moving.

That's why White and Epston's work in narrative therapy is so important – by recognising we can choose alternative narratives, we can re-author our lives.[7] To borrow from the movie world again, when we think about how our archetype or character fits within these grand master storylines, we can discover alternative scripts we can step into.

Here's a quick example. Instead of thinking about yourself as 'broken' or 'stuck', you can begin shifting towards a positive, empowering identity. For example, "I'm a helper, and I'm becoming a mentor."

To lean on Christopher Vogler's work in *The Writer's Journey*, archetypes give us a language of possibility and hope. We start to discover who we can become. New empowering roles open up for us.[8]

So, let's take a look at some of the archetypes that can help us on this journey of rewriting the stories we tell ourselves.

FIND YOURSELF IN THE STORY

When we talk about rewriting our stories, our first instinct is to think only in abstract terms: "I'll be more confident" or, "I'll show up differently." But one of the most powerful ways to gain clarity is to borrow from something we already know well from popular forms of storytelling like movies and TV series: characters and how they evolve. That's where the *Codebreaker Archetypes* come in.

These archetypes help you see yourself as a character in your own narrative. They give you the language to name the qualities, challenges and opportunities in front of you. Some of these archetypes might describe who you are now; others might describe who you're becoming. And quite likely, you'll see yourself in more than one because our lives are messy, complex and often don't fit neatly into predefined boxes.

And yet when we look at the world of personal narratives, it's not hard to identify with and relate to the characters we enjoy in books, films, theatre and myths. Quite often, they mirror our lived experience, and there's a cathartic moment when you realise, *I'm just like that character*. That's because good storytellers and directors know they do more than just entertain. Stories are a type of mirror. When you sit in a cinema or turn the pages of a novel, part of what grips you is you see yourself – your doubts, your hopes, your contradictions – all reflected in the characters on the screen or page.

However, those moments produce feelings that run deeper than simple catharsis. Our personal identities are the product of a life well-lived – they're never constructed in isolation. We tell ourselves who we are using the same story archetypes and narratives that have echoed through human history: the hero, the mentor, the fool, the explorer, the phoenix rising from ashes.

The Codebreaker Archetypes we're about to discuss in detail aren't prescriptions – they're invitations to discover more about who you are and who you're becoming. Which of the following archetypes resonates with you most? Which one do you instinctively resist? Both answers tell you something important about the story you're living.

The Hero

The Hero is on a quest. This is the central character, the one we root for, the one who lays the path ahead. The Hero embodies growth, drive and the possibility of transformation.

In leadership or workplace storytelling, the Hero is often a senior leader within the team, the CEO or anyone in the company who steps up and rescues the organisation from a difficult situation. A key insight when reflecting on the Hero archetype, or lead character, is to recognise you're on a journey – not at the end. A deep understanding of where you and the team are on this journey can deliver meaningful insights. For example, all heroes in stories that conform to Joseph Campbell's hero's journey storytelling model find themselves in tricky or even desperate situations. The good news is the hero always recovers, against all odds. That idea alone can give you hope in dark times.

NARRATIVE INSPIRATION

The Hero's Journey. Luke Skywalker leaving Tatooine. Frodo setting out from the Shire. Ordinary people stepping into extraordinary challenges.

The Mentor

The Mentor is the director of their own and others' stories. They're the vision setter, the guide, the one who offers wisdom, encouragement or performance notes at the right time. They see the big picture and help connect the dots.

Think Gandalf, Yoda or Dumbledore – characters who remind the hero of their purpose and keep the strategy on track. In leadership, the Mentor is often a coach, a senior leader or sometimes that inner voice that reframes your limiting beliefs into empowering truths. These are people with years of experience and wisdom who seem to share it effortlessly in both formal and informal settings.

Reflecting on your role as a Mentor can help you become more intentional and careful about what you say to whom, and when. Your words matter. On the other hand, if you're receiving wisdom from someone you consider a Mentor, open your ears, so to speak. Ask questions, value their wisdom and take action if needed.

NARRATIVE INSPIRATION

The Hero's Journey and recovery communities where people who've walked through fire help others do the same.

The Navigator

A Navigator is a friend, supporter or team member who makes things happen. They embody community and shared effort. They bring dreams to life with clarity and determination.

In business, the Navigator might be that colleague who always steps up or a peer who offers encouragement. Within families, they provide stability during upheaval or seasons of change.

Navigators love helping people. For them, acts of service are one of their primary love languages. Keen to avoid the spotlight, they revel in the shadows with key supporting roles.

NARRATIVE INSPIRATION
The Hero's Journey and purpose-driven storytelling. Navigators remind us that no one succeeds alone.

The Futurist

The Futurist sees obstacles and dangers before others do – but also opportunities. They're people who announce that change is coming: "Your old world is over. Here's the call to adventure." In my world of professional speaking, the classic version of this are futurists who speak about new and emerging technologies. They observe connections and patterns, applying wisdom and research to make predictions about how our lives will change.

The Futurist can also be a visionary leader who helps everyone see the way forward – an ideal partner for the Hero. Bold, insightful and exacting. Futurists are important because they bring hope, optimism and endless possibilities.

NARRATIVE INSPIRATION
The guardian in the Hero's Journey, the phoenix rising from the ashes and stories of continuous growth.

The Optimist

The Optimist is the character who brings humour, disruption and lighthearted energy to crises. They challenge assumptions, think differently and make the ordinary memorable.

Like Seinfeld noticing the quirks of daily life, or the comic sidekick in a blockbuster, the Optimist helps make the unbearable bearable. They're people who know that the circumstances are bad, but they dare to look beyond the moment and help others gain a hopeful or realistic perspective.

In leadership stories, the Optimist is the one who asks: "Why not?" Sometimes bold and out the front, other times a quiet team player who steps up to encourage teams at the right times. What's not to love about the Optimist?

NARRATIVE INSPIRATION

The Hero's Journey, rags-to-riches tales and the comic relief in almost every film you love.

The Critic

The Critic represents the darker side of storytelling: the villain, the antagonist, the destructive force. In personal narratives, the Critic shows up in burnt-out, disengaged people. It can also be found in toxic cultures where it's not safe to speak positively. The Critic revels in a climate of cynicism.

However, the Critic isn't always obvious. They can be charming, genial, even helpful. But underneath, they sap energy and derail progress. At work, they're the person who others accommodate.

People avoid giving them certain types of work, and entire teams can find themselves constructing elaborate workarounds to prevent the Critic from getting in the way. Who likes the Critic? Perhaps only other Critics!

NARRATIVE INSPIRATION

Contamination and turning point stories - the moment when one event ruins everything unless the character finds a way to rise above. Think Uncle Rico in *Napoleon Dynamite* or the cynic who always explains why something won't work.

The Phoenix

In storytelling, the rising phoenix is a well-known symbol of optimism. A fiery (near) death experience and rebirth. Think Ancient Greek and Roman mythology – they linked the sun's rising each day to the idea that light follows darkness.

The Phoenix is strong, courageous and inspiring. By definition, they've experienced some form of crisis, suffering or devastating hardship that forced them to take stock of everything.

Leaders who've recovered from losses, company collapse or tragic circumstances may identify with the Phoenix archetype – partly due to the hardship, but critically because it speaks to the power of rewriting your narrative with hope, resilience and renewed clarity. These are people who understand the highs and lows of life at a deeper level, and when they're at their best, they lead with a depth of insight and clarity that transforms teams and entire organisations.

NARRATIVE INSPIRATION

The 'death and rebirth' in the Hero's Journey and recovery narratives where adaptability is survival.

DECODE YOUR CHARACTER

Which Codebreaker Archetypes fits your current character? Are you partway through your Hero's journey, answering the call to adventure? Or are you slipping into the mindset of the Critic due to overwork and burnout?

Once you've determined your Codebreaker Archetype (you could be a combination of several), it's time to reflect and decide how to script your new lead character. Maybe nothing needs to change. Maybe *everything* needs to change. More likely, you'll land somewhere in the middle.

So, let's reflect on your Codebreaker Archetype:

- How do you feel about your archetype? Do you want to change it, or keep it?
- What new ideas, insights or challenges come to mind about your journey when reflecting on your archetype?
- What connections can you see between one or more archetypes and the voice of your inner critic and any limiting beliefs you hold?
- What does your new lead character look like? Which archetypes do they embody?

Take a moment to write down or make a voice recording of your thoughts in free form. Don't think too much. Just respond to the ideas and feelings generated by thinking about the connections between your self-talk and identity.

Researcher, author and inner speech expert Francesco Fanti Rovetta says our 'personal narrator' constructs the coherent and meaningful story of our lives.[9] I love this perspective – because we can start to develop a director's eye for the big picture.

THE POWER OF ARCHETYPES

Each of the Codebreaker Archetypes has roots in classic story structures we've inherited from myth, theatre and film.

The **Hero** is everywhere in movies: Barbie, Frodo in *Lord of the Rings*, Luke Skywalker in *Star Wars* and Evelyn Wang in

Everything All at Once. Not always heroic, they can find themselves drawn into a story – a grand drama where their help is required. They're a mix of vulnerability, empathy and bravery.

We see the **Mentor** in *Karate Kid* and *Babylon* – a chaotic movie about 1920s–30s Hollywood. The character Jack Conrad (Brad Pitt) is a mentor to Manny Torres (Diego Calva). Manny also becomes a mentor as he rises through the system.

The **Navigator** helps people stay grounded, a stabilising force amid crisis and change. In *The Other Me,* the character Irakli meets someone who helps him interpret visions, which grounds him in identity and truth.

The **Futurist** balances risk and resilience. In *Dune: Part Two*, characters like Paul Atreides (Timotheé Chalamet) foresee consequences, paths and omens of what's to come. We're drawn to these characters who can see multiple possible futures and help us move forward with intention and clarity.

The **Optimist** reminds us of what's possible and often does so with energy or humour. The characters Rocket and Groot in *Guardians of the Galaxy Vol. 3* are classic examples.

The **Critic**, our antagonist, can be a useful counterpoint to excessive optimism, but ultimately becomes destructive without intervention. The incredible *Oppenheimer* features a number of characters who warn that the project will fail – necessary for drama and tension in the movie, and also reflective of real life.

Finally, the **Phoenix** archetype reminds us that

transformation and recovery from suffering are possible – even when that character is flawed or imperfect. Phoenix stories captivate us with the possibility of rebirth, whether it's Wakanda's mourning of T'Challa in *Black Panther: Wakanda Forever* or Peter Parker rising from near-collapse in *Spiderman: No Way Home*.

When you reflect on your own life, which of these characters feels familiar? Which Codebreaker Archetype is closest to your experience? This isn't about choosing a permanent identity, but about naming the chapter you're currently in. Because once you see yourself as a character in a story, you can begin to author the next act with your inner coach and healthy beliefs in mind.

DECIDE – REWRITE YOUR STORY

(PART ONE)

DECODE YOUR CURRENT STORY

"New story, new life,
endless possibilities."

The days and weeks following my 2019 panic attack were a blur. A couple of weeks off work and the hazy days of COVID-19 lockdowns turned my world upside down. Few things felt normal.

A seemingly unremarkable turning point came at my local GP's office when he recommended a psychologist. I didn't know it at the time, but many people find it hard to find a 'good' therapist. That is, they don't like the person, or there isn't a great fit. I suspect for some people, it's unlikely anyone is a good fit at this stage of their mental health crisis – it's not like they're in the right mindset to make great decisions! But for me, something began to click as my sessions with Tim unfolded. In simple terms, I was in denial. He confirmed that I was, in fact, depressed. I had trouble getting my head around this diagnosis. My inner narrative was still fixed on the idea that *other* people had depression. I'd seen it many times over in close circles. I'd visited people in hospital wards and seen inside those small, confronting, white rooms.

Turns out I'd seen myself as an eternal Optimist meets Hero. I believed my life was supposed to keep tracking onwards and upwards without the inevitable drama! Other people had problems. But for me, life was supposed to keep getting better and better. It was an idea reinforced over the years by friends cheering me and Heather on in our life and business – from the outside, four children and a growing founder-led business are great success markers. A happy, largely untroubled childhood with incredibly loving, stable parents had set a template that didn't account for any major hurdles. No one's fault, it's just that your family environment, whatever it is, tends to set your expectations for the decades to follow. Well, it turns out this continuous growth narrative was wrong – deceptive, even.

> **Reflecting on my journey, I've come to realise
> the gap between my expectations of how
> life *should* be and the reality of what I was
> experiencing had grown as the years wore on.**

A fracture had emerged between this subconscious expectation and the brutal, biological reality. Fears about the future led to anxiety, which I carried for years as a business owner. This anxiety fuelled sustained, underlying stress that, in turn, manifested in a mental and physical breakdown.

As we all know, the truth of the matter is that life is a messy mix of different emotions and experiences. Most, if not all, the narratives and archetypes we've been exploring in this chapter can apply to each of us at different times or in different seasons of life.

In my case, I'd not stopped to seriously consider there was a healthier way of thinking about my experiences. I'd not yet cracked the Story Code.

THE VISION REALITY GAP

A simple model that illustrates the tension I was feeling, and applies to all of us at different times, is the Vision Reality Gap.

I wrote about it in *Beliefonomics* as a way of describing how audiences can interpret the messages and stories told by brands and an organisation's leadership.

The Vision/Reality Gap

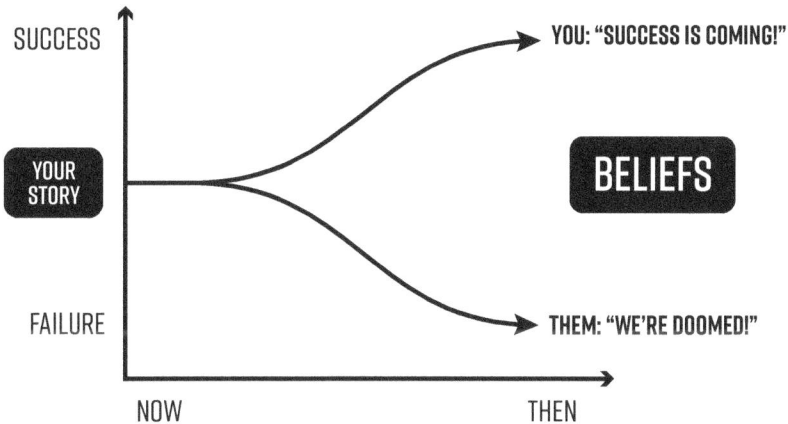

Here's a quick example. In public settings, usually at work, the Vision Reality Gap plays out when a leader speaks about the future. They cast a future vision – the growth we'll achieve to-gether and the clients we'll win. Picture a motivational talk at a sales kick-off. The CEO says, "We can do this, team! Let's go!"

From experience, it's quite common in the US. When I was living in San Francisco as a journalist and news editor at *InfoWorld Magazine* in the early 2000s, I heard my fair share of motivational pep talks. I'll never forget hearing the then CEO at *InfoWorld* tell us not to worry about the freshly popped dotcom bubble. It was early 2000, and the NASDAQ had just tanked spectacularly. The world was in turmoil (what's changed?), so our team of a few hundred people had gathered to hear from our leadership.

"It's okay, I've seen these things before. They come and go, so we'll be okay," our CEO said. His vision was, in essence, that we would survive.

The harsh reality was quite different. As journalists out there talking with analysts and business leaders, we very quickly realised this stock market crash was no mere blip. The steady stream of dotcoms advertising in our magazine was quickly disappearing. Websites had sprung up tracking the number of companies going bust *each day*. Our CEO's 'vision' that we'd be okay was very much detached from reality. In fact, reflecting on this season was one of the aha moments that sparked the idea for this book – as mentioned, many of the storytelling tools, techniques and methods I've taught people to use in external settings apply equally to our internal narratives, the stories we tell ourselves.

As leaders, one of our greatest opportunities for personal growth and development is firstly gaining awareness of these stories, then rewriting them with positive intent.

The deeper we understand our stories through the lens of our archetypes and personal narratives, the better equipped we'll be to manage change.

In my case, I was completely ill-equipped to understand why my body reacted against sustained stress. I remember telling Tim, "I *just can't believe* I'm depressed." I hated loud noises, crowds and lived in fear of another panic attack, and there was little I could do to control this new biological reality.

Contrast my situation with that of Steve Vamos, one of Australia's most successful tech sector CEOs. He has led the local operations of Apple, Microsoft and NineMSN and was successful in his role as CEO at Xero. I'd interviewed him a few times in my journalist days, and we've stayed in touch over the years.

When we caught up during my research for this book, Steve spoke about running NineMSN, a now defunct online platform that ran between 1997 and 2013. Joining the company with little direct experience in advertising – the platform's main source of revenue – was daunting. But it wasn't an overwhelming experience. Healthy leaders with a clear perspective on life generally know how to adapt and change. "Not knowing the business was a blessing because it forced me to focus on making everyone more effective, rather than trying to be the advertising expert."

In fact, Steve has led teams through a variety of 'shifts and shocks' over the years and even wrote a book titled *Through Shifts and Shocks: Lessons from the Front Line of Technology and Change*. He journeyed through the mini computing era, cloud computing, financial crises, workforce reductions at companies like IBM and the onset of the AI era. Steve explained:

> I've come to believe that human beings are not naturally good at change, and that meaningful change happens through teamwork and collaboration. Unfortunately, too many teams aren't performing to their potential, which is concerning in our world of accelerating and unpredictable change. We need to get better at change, both individually and collectively.

It's easy to read his words and nod silently. Of course, humans aren't good at change – *other humans*, we think. Perhaps my mental programming as a journalist made me always think in abstract ways, silently 'othering' people and not fully appreciating I was also part of the 'other'.

I asked Steve about his perspective on life and work now that he's working at arms-length from these companies that dominated his life.

My belief is that your beliefs define you and your
actions. The story you tell yourself informs your
beliefs, which then define your actions, leading to
either positive or negative outcomes. At NineMSN,
I quickly received positive feedback on my management style because fixing small things had a big
impact, making people believe I was making things
better for them. I was also confident that online
advertising would be huge. My naivety was an
advantage because the experts were sceptical. My
simple logic was: ads pay on TV and in newspapers, so why wouldn't they pay on this new device?

Great advice for any leader. Yet he wasn't perfect, and business
life wasn't always smooth sailing.

Meeting Kerry Packer was an experience. When
I complimented him on their support, he wasn't
interested in pleasantries and wanted to get straight
to business. It reminded me of another moment
with Steve Jobs at the first offsite meeting when he
was interim CEO. I suggested he visit Australia,
and he was quite blunt in his dismissal of the idea.
Initially taken aback, I rationalised it by thinking
he was focused on saving the company. These
experiences taught me that my upbringing instilled

in me a self-confidence that allowed me to respond okay in such situations. Your beliefs and sense of self are crucial. When dealing with senior people who react strongly, often it's triggered by something from their past. I even had a team member at Microsoft tell me in front of 500 people that what I was saying was nonsense, and I appreciated it because honest feedback is essential for progress. In such moments, taking a breath and not taking things too personally is key to avoid triggering your worst self.

While it might seem from the outside that I've always had it together, my journey has included pain and serious self-doubt, even now as an author. Impostor syndrome is real for me. I recall losing a significant deal at IBM, which cost me sleep for days. My time on the David Jones board was particularly challenging due to investor issues, which impacted me personally, feeling like I wasn't performing as well as I could. So, despite some successes, I am definitely a work in progress, with moments of self-doubt even today, both professionally and personally.

In response, Steve has talked about bringing more discipline to his life. Doing yoga a few times a week to clear his head and walking 10,000 steps each day with music. Eating well. Sleeping well. Learning about breathwork and remaining focused on personal growth.

Critically, he adopted a 'learn-it-all' approach to life rather than become a 'know it all'. It set him up to live in a healthy, open and accessible way in contrast to many of the people he knew in his professional circles who struggled with a victim mentality – or the contamination narrative I've mentioned.

It's a great story that combines self-awareness, courage and the ability to connect the dots between different events in one's career.

CODEBREAKING TO CONNECT THE DOTS

The irony for me is I'd long prided myself on being great at connecting the dots. Our first company, Filtered Media, was named after an idea that clients value people who can connect the dots. It's a core skill in journalism and highly valued in corporate circles. The trouble is each of us is too close to our own story.

> **It takes focus, attention and a degree of humility to accept that the personal narrative you're carrying might not actually reflect reality.**

On the upside, gaining clarity and insights in this area feels like a proper breath of fresh air. Over the past 2 years, I've come to realise I'm inhabiting a recovery narrative. I'm no longer in crisis or dealing with the existential crisis of not conforming to the constant growth narrative. The archetypes that most strongly resonate are *Futurist* and *Optimist* – the latter particularly gratifying because it feels like a return to form. In simple terms, it's a new mindset that has allowed me to fully embrace a long list of positive steps that support the recovery process. Like Steve's example, I've leant heavily into what mental health experts call the basics: eating, sleeping and exercising. I'm working with a naturopath to address some deficiencies caused by years of poor food choices. I've got a personal trainer who has helped me overcome the mental block of going to the gym – I no longer need to think about what exercises to do. I just do what I'm told as part of a structured program, and it's paying dividends. Likewise, I'm now getting more consistent, quality sleep, and I'm out regularly, almost daily, walking the dog. Spiritually, I'm also more engaged and connected to my faith than at any point in the last decade.

The result? Energy to burn. Momentum. Focus. We moved house recently, and I worked for 10 to 12 hours per day like a machine – moving boxes, unpacking, taking junk to the tip. I'm 51, and I had the energy of my 30-something self.

My return to optimism and serving my family is also hugely gratifying. I'm dreaming about new business ideas and how I can encourage leaders to live their best lives.

Go back a few years, and none of that was my reality. I've used the Story Code to closely examine the stories I tell myself and ask hard questions about what's needed in each area of life to turn them around.

EXPLORE YOUR PERSONAL NARRATIVE

One of the remarkable aspects of narrative therapy is its ability to help fuel this journey from self-doubt and crisis to self-confidence and wellbeing. It positions ordinary people like you and me as experts in our own stories. We have worthy, insider knowledge about our lives that's honoured and explored as a pathway to health and recovery.

David Newman, the psychologist at Sydney Narrative Therapy I introduced earlier, told me about his experiences working with people of all ages who were experiencing self-doubt, mental health issues or feeling like they were stuck in a rut.

He explained that honouring a person's lived experiences is powerful because it helps them discover the layers or stories hidden beneath the surface. Problem stories are those most often discussed in therapy sessions – the stresses and strains of life that are causing suffering. Yet in the "shadows of the problem story" is a new story that begins to emerge as you explore and begin to rewrite your narrative. David explained:

Quite often, whatever is in the shadows is preferred. It might well be the story of some self-confidence in the face of self-doubt. It might well be a story of how to deal with depression that is close to the depression story.

Clearly, what David is talking about here is central to our idea of unlocking the Story Code. Within the shadows of our problem story is a *contrasting* story – the opposite and often positive take on your personal narrative that has been lost, hidden or forgotten. He labelled these new, shadow stories as inherently "thin" because they feel tentative and weak. We're not sure if we believe fully in our own ability. Racked with self-doubt, the idea that you have the capacity to be strong and capable can feel like a distant possibility. David explained further:

New stories get strength by being witnessed by others, being retold by others. So that's often spoken of as witnessing. It can be incredibly powerful in strengthening new stories.

In this context, the witnessing role is performed by a therapist – they're not the "meaning makers," as David explained to me. However, in other therapeutic contexts, we can expect to be told what's wrong.

Now, unpacking this idea is also possible in personal and

professional settings. As you've no doubt experienced over a coffee with friends or colleagues, having someone validate your story – both the problem story and the new story emerging from the shadows – is incredibly powerful.

SO WHAT? PRACTICAL TECHNIQUE TO DEFINE AND LIVE YOUR NEW STORY

To help you shape your new narrative, here's a storytelling technique I teach clients in keynotes and workshops that will help you latch onto the positive moments in your personal history and go even deeper. Think of it as a simple approach to fleshing out your story so you can easily remember it during moments of stress or difficulty.

I'm talking about the Three S's of Storytelling: Setup, Surprise, So What.

All stories have three basic elements, and no, it's more than beginning, middle and end.

- **Setup**: The who, what, why, when. All the details, facts and curious ideas that set the scene.
- **Surprise**: The twist, a delight or unexpected drama in your story. Maybe it's a moment that causes you to think twice because it is indeed a surprise.
- **So what**: The final chapter in your story begs the question … *So what?* Why should *you* care about your own story? Why should *anyone* care?

So what? is the one aspect of personal storytelling I've found people most often overlook. We're very happy to tell friends or colleagues all about the details of our holiday to Fiji, for example. We'll describe the beach, the hospitality and probably spend too much time talking about the weather – *of course* you were surprised it rained the whole time!

The big question is, *so what?* What did your holiday to Fiji mean to you? Was it even better than you imagined despite the rain? Or were you so miserable it taught you some other valuable lesson?

So what? answers those questions. The difference here is you're taking time to answer those questions for yourself, the audience of one. You're learning to lean into the positive stories of an inner coach instead of that debilitating inner critic. As we know, sometimes we must write a whole new narrative.

LOOKING FORWARD TO YOUR FUTURE STORY

Our personal narratives are sometimes conscious, and at other times, part of our subconscious understanding of the world. It might be that, in reading to this point, you're starting to identify some of the problem stories, or 'issues', that are feeding your inner critic, limiting beliefs, and causing you to reflect on your Codebreaker Archetype. As you decipher more of the Story Code, your new narrative begins to emerge.

Before we move on to the next chapter, I'll leave you with a parting thought on the power of narratives in our lives and, more broadly, society.

I watched a fascinating episode of a Netflix documentary series called *The Mind, Explained*. The episode is titled 'Brainwashing', and it explores the cryptology of cults, belief systems and the stories we're told about grand narratives in society.

Intuitively, we know that our culture, leaders, media and other sources of storytelling shape how we think, feel and act. As tribal people, we use storytelling to reinforce and support our groups. Our beliefs and personal narratives are intertwined. We want to belong, and so we're invited to join grand narratives that unite and sometimes divide. "Oftentimes these narratives, they have a particular goal, which is to cast the powers of society or the world into a negative light and to cast you as a revolutionary who can change it all … It makes you the Luke Skywalker of this hero's journey," the documentary explains.[1]

Of course, this is just one storyteller's take on how macro narratives in society and our own internal narratives collide. What is true, however, is we often embody the narratives of our tribes at work, in our cities, nations and various faith and cultural groups without too much conscious analysis. It's typically during moments of crisis when the gulf between our vision and reality – the internal narrative and the external reality – becomes so wide we start to ask big questions. Whether or not we see ourselves as a hero, victim or innocent bystander in these stories, we're inevitably drawn into a deep sense of conviction that something's not right. Our inner story seems out of sync with the world around us, and it's way less than comfortable.

Sure, denial is an option. You can choose to ignore the inner tension. But as my example and those of others experiencing self-doubt and burnout attest, you can only carry this burden for so long before your body gives out.

CHAPTER 8

DECIDE – REWRITE YOUR STORY
(PART TWO)

WRITE YOUR NEW NARRATIVE

"Successful leadership begins with knowing what gives you energy, optimism and hope for the future."

All movies, novels and great stories through the ages have some element of surprise. It could be drama, or something happy and amazing. Whatever it is, it's unexpected. You didn't see it coming. When using the Story Code to unlock new ideas, emotions and narratives, they often come as a surprise because we're too close to our own stories.

In comedy, they call this surprise the 'twist' or 'punchline'. Comedians deliver a set-up – the beginning of a story. Then comes the punchline or twist. It's funny because expectations are altered. You think the joke is going one way, but surprise! It goes the other way. Comedy is a great template for storytelling because all stories need a surprise and some element of drama and tension. A story without drama is no story at all. It's a pointless narrative.

That idea alone is challenging for many leaders and corporations. If you're busy selling your vision and why your products or services are unique, drama isn't typically part of the story. That is, we don't market ourselves and our products by leading with our weaknesses or struggles. But here's the twist for you and your journey from self-doubt to success – you're writing your new story for an audience of one. You! Ignoring the drama is to put aside the tension, stress and reality of life in a way that's self-deceptive.

One point of wisdom worth drawing on here is a practice in First Nations mobs. Mark Yettica-Paulson comes from the Kamilaroi, Bundjalung and Bera peoples on the New South

Wales-Queensland border – which makes the State of Origin NRL contests a bit tricky! Yet this complexity has taught him the value of understanding family histories and the 'false lines' we put around state and local borders. First Nations people see themselves as interrelated to their human families and more broadly connected to all types of kin: plant, animal, sea, sky and land. They're not 'on country' but 'in country' in the sense of being connected to it more deeply than the Western mindset typically allows.

Within this context, Mark spoke about something both Aboriginal leaders and narrative practitioners value – telling the whole story. Not just the highs, but the painful truths of history, which we know are well-documented in the Australian story. Embracing and valuing survival, and preserving culture and hope are just as much a part of First Nations storytelling as traditional storytelling. Mark explained:

> You can claim a sense of that displaced or uprooted belonging by saying, "I am from these people, my parents, my grandparents, my great grandparents." I can carry that story with me wherever I go so that, along with this inherited thing of we navigate through tensions, we don't navigate through certainties. That has really helped me to not get overwhelmed.

It must take extraordinary grace and humility to embrace the stories of trauma and displacement that are part of First Nations family histories. For Mark and his mob, it has been a journey of deliberately choosing to accept the drama while emphasising the hopeful stories in preference to those of despair.

> My ancestors helped provide a language by saying
> transformation is where hope and despair meet.
> And I was like, "That's how I've been carrying a lot
> of this stuff." You know, it's desperately hopeless,
> but it is also hopeful at the same time.

BRING YOUR NEW STORY INTO THE LIGHT

In Western culture, we often focus on negative stories at work and in our personal lives. We move fast. In fact, our whole society and economic system is geared around speed and productivity. Being 'busy' is still a badge of honour, even in these post-COVID days when many people have settled into new, slightly less-intense lifestyles.

Mark often hears executives in leadership programs say they feel torn, saying things like, "I know I'm not giving one hundred percent. I feel like I'm giving less of me in all of these spaces that are competing for my attention." He said it impacts our ability to hold on to our stories.

And so comes the challenge. Often, in our journeys, our problem stories still loom large, and they're constantly reinforced. To move forward and inspire hope, you must separate your problem story from your 'shadow story', or 'preferred story', bringing it into the light.

UNLOCK THE VAULT THAT HOLDS YOUR NEW STORY

Let's dive deeper and more thoroughly decipher the Story Code to unlock your ideal story.

Here's an encouragement as we get going. Rewriting your story isn't some wistful self-help mumbo jumbo. There's cryptology at play. We're actually rewiring your brain to focus on that shadow story, the hidden version of yourself that has been overshadowed by the problem story. Isn't that wild?

Studies show that writing about past experiences, especially emotional ones, helps us process them in a healthier way and improves psychological wellbeing.[1] People who use expressive writing to process traumatic events can experience reductions in PTSD, depressive symptoms, and negative self-talk and even improve their physical wellbeing.[2]

At this point, one of the biggest strategic levers you can pull is to begin gathering evidence of your own success. Positive stories from your own life are incredibly powerful because our brains are wired for negativity. We remember failures more than successes because, evolutionarily speaking, doing so helped us survive. You were more likely to stay alive if you remembered *not* to touch fire than if you remembered a lovely meal.

But these days, this hardwired bias works against us. Many people are stuck in a negative loop – it can easily feel like the world is spinning out of control, as negative stories are constantly reinforced through social platforms. There's almost too much to comprehend. No wonder more people are choosing to tune out of the news cycle. When you think about this at scale, it's not hard to understand why many workplaces are unhealthy. Low morale, poor productivity and limited performance are signals of low psychological safety. And all this despite many HR leaders and senior managers recognising they assume a great responsibility for the mental wellbeing of employees in today's workplace.[3]

So, back to the evidence. Why does it matter? The simple reason is you can't easily lie to yourself. Motivational quotes don't hit home unless they tap into personal experience, stories or facts about your life you know to be true. Therefore, gathering evidence isn't a process of finding flimsy stories that bolster fake affirmations that ring true for someone else. It's about finding proof from your life that matters to you. We're looking for real evidence from your past that proves you're capable, strong and ready for change.

PENS READY? COMMENCE!

Let's go through a detailed version of the Three S's of Storytelling, plus three additional steps to help make your story memorable:

1. **Setup**: Gathering facts and evidence
2. **Surprise**: What's unique about this story?
3. **So what**: What's the one point, or care factor?
4. **Draft**: Rewrite your story
5. **Re-read, edit, reflect**: Polish your story
6. **Publish**: Memorise and embed your new story in your mind by publishing

Sounds easy, right? Sort of. The hard work happens when you're confronted with the reality of your inner narrative. Rewriting your story requires commitment, bravery and a determination to see it through. Your boss, friend, partner or parent isn't going to hold you to account unless you ask them!

And remember as you go through these steps, rewriting your story isn't a silver bullet, nor is it an instant fix. We'll talk later about setting expectations around timelines. We'll also discuss various options to move you forward on your healing journey in the best way possible.

So, let's make this happen.

Step 1: Setup – Gathering Facts and Evidence

First get clear on each segment of the Story Code we've covered so far: challenging your inner critic, overwriting limiting beliefs and scripting a new lead character, and defining your personal narrative. Once you've cracked the code, you start to get an idea of what's possible – ideas, dreams, a vision for a future you. Who are you becoming? And critically, why does this new narrative matter to you? A picture begins to emerge. The opposite of the negative narrative holding you back.

Still processing? If so, go back and review the previous chapters.

With the context of writing your new story in mind, spend time reflecting on past successes, wins and unexpected changes in fortune. Write down all the facts and evidence you can remember or dig up from your archives (emails, photos, social media, news clippings, awards). If it helps, you can borrow an old technique from journalism, the five W's and the H: *who, what, where, when, why and how.* That is, ask yourself: *Who was there? What happened? Where were you? When did this happen? Why did it happen? And how did you respond?*

Now, some people have difficulty finding real-life examples that contradict their old stories, so here are a few headline ideas to get you thinking:

- I led a successful project last year.
- I have strong, supportive friendships.
- I've navigated difficult situations successfully before.

A few more practical ideas that can help include:

- Ask mentors, colleagues or friends what they see in you. If you're super modern, brave or vibey, ask ChatGPT or your AI of choice what it knows about you that you might not be aware of!
- Keep a journal of wins. Write down small and big achievements shortly after they happen. If my experience is a predictor, there's a good chance you'll forget them!
- Revisit old doubts. What did you once believe you couldn't do but eventually did?
- Look at your past wins. What have you achieved despite fear, uncertainty and self-doubt?

Step 2: Surprise – What's Unique About This Story?

Research reveals that when we reflect on our best moments – times we've succeeded, felt proud or overcome a challenge – our confidence grows, and negative self-talk shrinks.[4] It's not rocket science, but the key here is taking time to do this reflection.

To that end, the 'high-point exercise' is a powerful way of helping you identify what's truly unique about this story.

1. Think of a high-point moment in your life – personal or professional.
2. Write about it in detail: unpack the details captured in step one.

3. Next, ask yourself a hard question: *Do I believe this story?* Do you really believe you were successful or that this moment in time really mattered? The only person you have to convince is yourself!

4. Talk about this moment with someone you trust. Be honest about how it makes you feel. External processing helps reframe experiences and build resilience.[5]

5. Write down the truly surprising fact or element of this story – that one idea that quietly impresses you or elicits the most reaction from people.

Step 3: So What – What's the One Point, or Care Factor?

When it comes to telling stories in public settings, I teach people that 'so what' or the 'care factor' is the one single idea you want your audience to remember. The same applies here.

In effect, you're writing a one-liner for your inner coach. What does this story mean to you? Does it prove you have what it takes? Maybe the surprise factor really demonstrates that hard work pays off. Or perhaps it's a personal reminder that you're more resilient and courageous than you give yourself credit for.

Step 4: Draft – Rewrite Your Story

Now it's time to bring everything together by reflecting on the previous steps and the insights you gathered from other segments of the Story Code – your inner coach, healthy beliefs and personal archetype.

Get creative! Write down the ideas that come to mind when you consider the connections between each segment. For example:

- *My inner coach tells me I'm capable of leading with courage. That aligns with my healthy belief that setbacks are opportunities, not failures. When I combine that with my Mentor archetype, I see a new story emerging: I'm here to guide others through change while continuing to grow myself.*

- *My healthy belief says it's never too late to change. My inner coach reminds me of past times I've done hard things. Linking that with my Explorer archetype, my new story becomes: I am resilient, adaptable and ready to thrive in uncertainty.*

The goal is to weave these three threads into a single, coherent narrative – a short statement of who you're becoming and how you'll show up in the world. This is where the Story Code clicks into place: the critic loses power because you now have a unified story that's believable, empowering and lived, and your sense of self, future hopes and evidence of success collide. There's no hard and fast rule for exactly how to do this – creativity and free thinking don't thrive inside tiny boxes.

Here are some tips to get you going:

- Lead with an affirmation. What type of person are you? Lean on your personal values and beliefs, and insights from the myriad personality tests out there.
- Avoid jargon! You're writing *yourself* a letter. Be you. Feel it. Keep it simple so it sticks in your memory.
- Remember, touch on the first three segments of the Story Code – what your inner coach says most often, why your healthy beliefs matter and how your future self, your new lead character, shows up in the world.

Step 5: Re-Read, Edit, Reflect

In my journey, this stage took the longest – around 12 months! Everyone's journey is different. Mine was punctuated by career changes, family dynamics and my learner personality – I've been gathering so much evidence, research and data across such a wide range of sources that it's taken me time to forge this path largely on my own. So, as you re-read, edit and reflect, give yourself time and space. It's a bit like a home renovation – takes twice as long and costs twice as much as you expected! And by cost, that could be time, energy, emotion and of course therapy bills.

I'm no mindfulness expert; however, it's at this point that it's useful to explore which forms of reflection work best for you. Walking? Running? Time out in the country? Processing your thoughts out loud with a friend?

Step 6: Publish – Memorise and Embed Your New Story in Your Mind by Publishing

Now it's time to publish your new story. By publish, I don't mean bare your soul on LinkedIn. That said, if that's what you want to do, be my guest! Publishing is a mindset. You need a set of words, or perhaps something a little more creative like a picture, painting, poem or diagram, that communicates your story. Feelings, aspirations and dreams matter. Remember your audience of one – you. Are you going to put these words or ideas up in the home office? Write them on a whiteboard at home where you can reflect further?

Adult learning principles are at play here. Repetition and external vocalisation with trusted friends, colleagues and family are also incredibly valuable. Reading your story out loud is an incredible experience – it helps validate and embed this emerging narrative in your psyche.

Again, we're not playing mind games here. This isn't an exercise in false motivation or self-deception. This is a true picture of you – it just happens to be the new, rescripted, ideal version of you. New story, new life, *endless possibilities*.

So, where to next for those brave enough to lean into the drama that is the stories we tell ourselves? Once you've decided what your future story looks like, the next step is to encode the daily habits that will support you, your new lead character and your consciously crafted narrative.

CHAPTER 9

ENCODE - DAILY HABITS CHANGE EVERYTHING

"Almost everything in life is work, unless you're at the beach. So, choose your work carefully."

How many workshops and personal development courses have you done? How many self-help or leadership books have you read? If you're anything like me, a fair few. My general rule of thumb is to try and take away one core idea, or single action point, that will make a difference. However, the bigger challenge is maintaining that new idea, action or change consistently over time.

I've been fascinated by this idea now for years. Specifically, at ImpactInstitute, we talk about 'sustainable' social change. That is, when you work on a program that benefits people and communities, your goal isn't necessarily a short-term blip in wellbeing. You want to see long-term, positive and sustainable change. So what does that look like in this context?

Rewriting your story isn't a set-and-forget process. The best mindset is one that says, *I'm* constantly *rewriting my story*. Like Indigenous storytellers who remind their mob of Dreamtime stories, there's wisdom in staying connected to your own story as it unfolds.

There is, however, a twist. This process of transformation involves making a conscious choice about your focus. What stories are you choosing to remember? Are you deciding to bring that shadow, preferred story into the foreground? Are you making a conscious effort to document and remember real evidence of your success – stories that mean something to you and give you a lift when you need it most?

Like any form of behavioural change or habit development,

it's important to set your expectations right. This isn't a quick fix. Change is an ongoing process that requires dedication and effort. Without consistent reinforcement, old habits and beliefs can easily resurface.

This chapter focuses on the tools and strategies you can encode into your life to change *everything*, helping you move onwards and prevent your new story from fading away. Here's some inspo: each small step you take isn't just a token effort. You're creating a foundation for a healthier and more resilient lifestyle.

So let's delve into how you can make this new, empowering story your default setting and ensure it lasts for the long haul.

JOURNALLING – THE WRITING CONTINUES!

Oddly, I was never really into journals. I did have them, but used them sporadically. Other people, like my wife, continue journalling their entire lives. It turns out she has the better habit.

Our brains are naturally wired to prioritise threats over positive experiences. We're more likely to pay attention to our inner critic and limiting beliefs than those of our inner coach or healthy beliefs. Listening to those old negative stories is simply holding you back.

Happily, the neuroscience backs the idea of regular journalling as a way of counteracting our very human bias towards negativity. It helps you process emotions, reframe setbacks and strengthen self-belief.[1]

By regularly writing about your experiences, you can actively reinforce your new story and challenge negative thoughts. Once the ideas of your inner critic are exposed on paper or a digital journal, they start to lose power. I've felt this shift in my own life and heard it said among coaching clients.

So, here are a few journalling tips:

- Pay attention to big moments – for example, stepping outside your comfort zone, managing a familiar situation with new-found confidence. How did you feel when you embraced your rewritten narrative?
- Make it a daily habit, or do it as often as you can. Write:
  » Something you did well
  » An unexpected challenge you handled
  » Give yourself positive feedback – for example, describe the progress you're making
- Keep your new story handy – this vision of your new lead character where you're picturing yourself alive and well, thriving and giving. You could keep a copy in the front or back of your journal for easy reference or stick it up on the wall at home. The key is to take a moment from time to time to read this future story and compare it to the day's events – what's surprising, different or noteworthy?

An easy way to remember why journals matter is this business adage: *what doesn't get measured doesn't get managed!*

If your inner critic is flaring up and telling you journalling is a waste of time, arm your inner coach with a different story: journals play the long game. They're helping you keep track of your story by recording evidence of how you're changing. A healthy belief to foster from this process is you are indeed becoming the person you've imagined.

PRACTISE DEEP LISTENING – WHAT'S YOUR INNER CRITIC REALLY SAYING?

The next habit to foster is listening, an invaluable skill in its own right. There's no shortage of research and professional literature focused on the fine art and science of how to listen.

While it sounds obvious, getting better at listening helps you pay closer attention to your own reactions to various inputs and experiences. Experts talk about the value of taking time to slow your mind and observe your thoughts in real time. When a thought pops into your head, ask yourself, is this idea what you truly believe? Or can you let it go?

According to Pauline Oliveros, a pioneer in the field, "deep listening is listening in every possible way to everything to hear no matter what you are doing."[2]

Author and host of the *Deep Listening* podcast, Oscar Trimboli, speaks about five levels of listening:

1. Listen to **yourself**: be aware of your internal distractions and emotions to be fully present.
2. Listen to the **content**: focus on the actual words spoken by the other person.
3. Listen for the **context**: understand the background, circumstances and environment influencing the conversation.
4. Listen for what's **unsaid**: pay attention to non-verbal cues and underlying emotions.
5. Listen for **meaning**: grasp the deeper significance and implications of the speaker's message.[3]

Trimboli's point, which mirrors others in this field, is we can gain incredible insights by consciously choosing to pay attention to the wisdom that's all around us, using it to inform our thinking and leadership style.

I've literally conducted thousands of interviews in 30 years of professional life as a journalist, podcaster and agency owner. It's honestly one of my favourite things. I love hearing someone express deeply held ideas that change both of us in the process. And so I'll add this one tip I've made a natural habit. Spend more time thinking about what the person is saying in the moment, and less time thinking about your next question. The next question you need to ask will be quite obvious as you reflect on what you've heard. Granted, it takes some practice to do this in real time!

In the context of listening to your inner critic, practising deep listening is powerful. What's it *really* saying? Over time, you'll spot the mistruths very quickly.

BEWARE OF SPEED BUMPS, BIG AND SMALL

Something I've noticed about speed bumps on the road is they're all different. Some are quite flat – you barely need to slow down. They feel like a vague suggestion to limit your speed. Others threaten to remove chunks from underneath your car if you go too fast. They're aggressively large!

The point is: setbacks on your personal transformation journey are inevitable. Some big, some small. But remember our growth mindset mantra? You're not there *yet*.

This is when the stories and evidence gathered for your inner coach really matter. Faced with criticism from a colleague or client? It's just an issue. The key is to recall the stories that remind you failure or rejection isn't part of *your* story. The process takes a little mental gymnastics and does get easier over time.

> Your inner critic and limiting beliefs aren't easily
> buried. It takes a lot of good news over a long
> time to properly smother them in optimism.

Here are a few more approaches you can use when things get tough or you can't remember those great stories of success:

- **Read your journal**
  Flick back through past successes. This is when the power of rewriting your story comes into its own.
- **Rewrite the narrative in real time**
  Actively challenge and reframe negative thoughts as they arise. What's the exact opposite of that negative idea? Can you quickly remember at least one small example that proves the reframed belief is true?
- **Read your future story again**
  Tap back into the motivation and drive behind the decision to rewrite your story. Nothing like some fresh inspiration to navigate difficult times.

HARNESS THE POWER OF HEALTHY HABITS

James Clear's *Atomic Habits* is a modern-day classic – go read it if it's not yet on your radar! His core idea is powerful: lots of tiny, consistent and positive changes compound over time, like interest, to transform your habits and reshape your life.[4]

With that in mind, here's how I've incorporated new habits and self-care routines into daily life:

- I'll often ask myself, *Am I expecting any surprises or big opportunities today?* It's a great way of preserving mental energy for the moments that count, and it helps you get really excited by situations you know are squarely aligned with your new story (for me, that's keynote speaking and consulting gigs!).

- Begin each day by revisiting your new story and setting an intention to act in ways that support your vision for who you're becoming. It's a simple practice that reinforces your commitment to your new identity and guides your actions throughout the day.

- As the day goes on, take a mental snapshot of the good moments. For me, it's a simple process of invoking my inner coach: *Hey, Mark, this is so cool. Remember this moment!*

- Watch your words. Look for opportunities to replace complaint with gratitude, or criticism with kindness, for example. It's a slightly offbeat idea, but I believe we are what we say.

- *And*, not *but*. Building on the words idea, a shout-out to speaker and a mentor of mine, Lindsay Adams, who challenged me to replace 'but' with 'and' – the former creates barriers and resistance while the latter is positive and optimistic.

- Pay close attention to your workplace environment. Just like choosing your friends carefully, be very mindful of the physical and psychosocial spaces you occupy in your home office or workplace. I've got a very simple test: Does this place feel good? If not, figure out why.

• Speaking of choosing your friends, choose your friends and colleagues carefully! To the extent it's possible, spend more time with people who build you up, not tear you down.

Here are two reflection questions to help you encode game-changing habits in your life:

• What's one micro-habit that supports your new story?
• How can you make your empowering story easier to follow than the limiting one?

Some handy suggestions:

• **Morning reframing.** Take one line from your 'healthy belief' list and speak it aloud each morning.
• **Story evidence journal.** At the end of each day, note one moment that proves your new story true.
• **Belief anchors.** Create physical cues (a card in your wallet, a screensaver, a sticky note) that remind you of your chosen archetype.

Research in psychology and behavioural economics confirms that repetition, environment design and social reinforcement are the most reliable ways to shift belief systems over time.[5] In narrative therapy, this is often described as 'living documentation' – keeping your preferred story visible and alive in daily life.

LEAD THE PROCESS, LEAD THYSELF

The last point deserves special attention. Much has been said about the importance of leading yourself before leading others. Rewriting your story is an incredible act of self-leadership. It's also very grown-up! I tell my kids that the definition of adulthood is making yourself do hard things when nobody else will. That insight applies here, with a twist.

One of the lessons I learnt from researching and writing *Beliefonomics* was a quote I use often in keynotes. We humans are a messy and inconsistent bunch. In business, we love to think about our colleagues, clients and community as consistent and predictable. Newsflash, they're not.

> Most of our choices are not the result of careful
> deliberation … We live in the moment and thus
> tend to resist change, are poor predictors of future
> behavior, subject to distorted memory, and affected
> by physiological and emotional states of mind.[6]

That applies to you and me equally.

So, like an editor working on a book or magazine, you get to *lead* the process of writing your own story. It's a process likely driven by a desire to restore a sense of control and build confidence and resilience in all aspects of your life.

Just make sure you're not too hard on yourself during the process. Don't expect perfection, consistent wins or immediate success. That said, don't go too easy, either. You're playing the coach and a metaphorical striker on the soccer team at the same time. It takes focus – so don't give up.

When your new story is consistently lived out in small, meaningful ways, it doesn't have to compete with your old story. By encoding habits, you rewire your brain for hope, resilience and agency. You set yourself up for success.

CHAPTER 10

UNDERSTAND THE JOURNEY AHEAD

"Life is always moving onwards. The trick is remembering you control the direction and speed."

"Dad, when will we get there?"

We learn about setting expectations very early in life. I used to love telling the kids, "We'll get there in five minutes!" The reality was, of course, way different. Family road trips used to be an all-day affair where it was better to think in hours, not minutes.

But the minutes would tick by for young minds, and they'd pipe up again. "I thought you said we'd be there in five minutes!"

Now, here's something I didn't know when we had little babies. Nobody tells you just how fun it is to wind up your kids. It's at this point in the car trip you can rip out some classic dad lines like, "Ask a silly question, get a silly answer!" The real answer? There's a map on the dashboard with the countdown, of course.

By this chapter, the picture in my mind is a state where some, or all, parts of your future story have started to become reality. Regaining your energy, getting clarity and feeling excited about the future is honestly the best. And yet, there's a shadow side. What's next? Do you need to reset your expectations again in the future? In a word, yes.

I caught up with a colleague from our industry network, Nicola Nel, who founded a fabulous, award-winning PR and creative agency in Johannesburg called Atmosphere. A few years ago, she sold the business – the culmination of a long journey from self-doubt as a young journalist to successful entrepreneur. After the excitement of selling the business died down, reality set in.

> Letting go of Atmosphere was hard, because my identity was wrapped up in this business. I was Atmosphere. We were an award-winning business. We were known for our creativity. And that reflected on my self-esteem. I thought the business was me. So I had to find my own identity again.

Nicola's experience might not be your story, but it offers a valuable lesson – with success can come pain! One goal completed invites introspection, which can be challenging. In Nicola's case, leaning on her healthy beliefs helped kickstart a new chapter. She explained, "One of mine is that I flourish when there's a challenge, and I grow through challenges." It's an insight that led her to accepting a role as the head of a network of global PR agencies called PROI Worldwide, of which my organisation is a part.

A fresh challenge was the right choice. And at the same time, the experience reinforced a separate, personal identity around the value of kindness and becoming a more people-oriented leader. Less task-oriented and less perfectionist.

EMBRACE THE UNFOLDING NARRATIVE

Overcoming self-doubt, rediscovering your identity and building confidence isn't a linear journey, and it doesn't always come with a map (luckily, you have the Story Code to unlock your own unique path forward!). Living your new story requires intentional effort, the right mindset, clear expectations and a willingness to engage with new perspectives. Along the way, you can expect to start believing in your own capabilities in an honest, grounded way that doesn't feel like self-deceit. You can also expect more confidence, less self-doubt and growing leadership skills.

So how do we get there? What are the different approaches worth considering as you forge ahead on this journey to re-write the stories you tell yourself?

I'm often asked about how long it takes, who someone should work with and what it takes to succeed. It's not a simple path, but there are a few options to consider.

1. **On Your Own**

   If you're a disciplined, focused person, this could be for you. I've given you an outline, and self-guided efforts efforts like journalling, self-reflection and reading will help you make steady progress. The advantage is it's completely flexible. You can make journal entries on the bus, at night or in the morning over breakfast.

It does, however, require strong discipline and consistency.

If that's not your cup of tea, you have other options.

2. **Small Groups**

Hanging out with colleagues or peers from different backgrounds in structured or informal groups accelerates your growth. My small group coaching experience for leaders is called *Flip the Script*. The key to meeting in small groups is a shared experience helps people feel validated, gain new perspectives and get that touch of accountability to keep moving onwards. Whether it's with me or in any other setting, I'm a big fan of small groups because they're great for:

» **Peer support:** connecting with others who share similar experiences can reduce feelings of isolation and create a sense of belonging.

» **Shared learning:** you can learn from real-world experiences and develop strategies for overcoming self-doubt.

» **Accountability:** reporting your progress increases motivation and commitment to keep going when it feels tough.

» **Validation:** constructive feedback and

encouragement from your peers boosts confidence and delivers external validation, which for some is very powerful.

» **Diverse perspectives:** interacting with people from different backgrounds is the stuff of life. It broadens your understanding and exposes you to different thinking patterns.

3. Therapist or Coach

I'm a big fan of therapy! That's a sentence I wouldn't have written years ago. Curiously, therapy isn't completely normalised in corporate environments – and certainly not among my cohort of middle-aged men. And yet we're experiencing a mental wellbeing crisis that's compelling people to seek the wisdom and guidance of psychologists, leadership coaches and other professionals in this field.

A professional simply turning up isn't enough. They must be able to tell you something you don't know. What can they see that you can't? Naturally, you're too close to your own story. Always keep that in mind.

Working with a therapist who specialises in narrative therapy can help you explore the expertise and wisdom you didn't realise was just below the surface. Speaking from experience, most therapists bring non-judgemental account-ability to the conversation. There's nothing quite like watching your psychologist flicking back through *their notes* about your story and smiling as they tell you just how far you've come down the road!

In summary, each approach will give you different levels of support and engagement. Just be sure to pick the one that best fits your style, needs and commitment level. It's a bit like my experience with gyms – if your current one doesn't quite work for you, don't be afraid to try another one. And keep going until you get it right.

ARE WE THERE YET?

How long can you expect this journey of self-discovery and rewriting your story to take? To quote my mum, "How long's a piece of string?"

That said, there are a few timeframes worth considering that will help set your expectations.

Quick Wins: Just Weeks!

Within 4 to 8 weeks, you can expect to:

- **Externalise your issues.** Separating your personal identity from the problems or issues you're facing. People often experience breakthroughs or big ahas within the first few sessions of a coaching program, or within the first weeks of focused, self-guided work.

- **Clarify your future-self.** Writing about past successes and identifying positive stories that align with your future self can spark a quick shift in your mindset. For example, when I began externalising my problems as problems, and not my identity, it was a game changer. My sense of self shifted overnight as I started going back to core truths about who I was, not what I did.

Sustained Change: 1 to 3 months

- **Rewriting your personal narrative.** My coaching experience and research indicates that with consistent effort, you can reshape limiting beliefs within 6 to 12 weeks, particularly in career and relationship contexts.[1]
- **Breakthroughs with journalling and reflection.** Weekly writing exercises and intentional reflection accelerate your self-awareness and reinforce new healthy beliefs.
- Additional accelerators on this journey include reinforcing your new story or new personal narratives through the experience of group validation and sharing your story.

Deep Change: 6 to 12 Months or More

Consistent focus, the passage of time and regular touchpoints with professionals and groups do wonders. From experience, one of the biggest changes you can expect over this timeframe is the feeling of your story settling down. There's a sense of calm and contentment that follows the experience of letting the story of your future self settle, or to borrow from viticulture, mature like a fine wine.

This process is particularly relevant for people who have experienced complex trauma or face the challenges of working on deeply rooted beliefs. People with ingrained patterns of self-doubt obviously need more time and most likely the input of professionals across different physical, mental, spiritual and emotional areas.

INFLUENCING FACTORS

The following answers may seem obvious, but when people ask me about the variables, or the reasons the process takes different lengths of time, a few things spring to mind.

1. **Engagement level:** How regularly are you applying these ideas and techniques? Are you writing and reviewing your story regularly?
2. **Complexity of the issue:** The more ingrained the belief, the longer it may take to rewrite your story.
3. **Your team:** Network of supportive peers, family and/ or professionals will directly impact the length of your journey.

4. **Readiness for change**: Are you open and willing to be vulnerable and brave while confronting important issues around self-doubt and burnout? Nobody is making you do this!

Rewriting your story is a bit like those old choose your own adventure books. It's not linear – you can skip forward, or back. There are plenty of twists and turns. You can write it in one sitting, but cooler heads will take their time to let it sink in.

What's your appetite for change?

CHAPTER 11

DEFINE SUCCESS ON YOUR TERMS

"Success is like happiness – it happens. But it doesn't happen without understanding your story."

One thing we love about movies and, in fact, all forms of storytelling is a great ending. A great ending resolves the tension. It draws all the threads together to deliver that deep sense of satisfaction that comes from a story well told. And so, to this, the last chapter. I hope you're hopeful about the story you're rewriting about your future self. Maybe you've caught a glimpse into an exciting future that in some way mirrors the satisfaction of a well-made movie or compelling novel.

The good news is this isn't fanciful stuff. Mastering the Story Code and, in turn, your life and future is possible. Forgive the humble brag, but a participant in my small group coaching program, 'Flip the Script', described her experience as "transformational," explaining: "It reminded me that our past does not define us, but our willingness to own it can reshape everything."

How cool is that? The key word here is *willingness*. As you rewrite the stories you tell yourself, a picture of your future self begins to emerge. A picture of how your life will be, how you will feel and what you'll be doing. But you must be willing to make it happen. You must be committed to gathering evidence of past successes and determined enough to connect the dots between those unforgettable moments in time. It's not a question of talent or ability. As we learn from narrative therapy, you're already the expert in your own life.

However, I'm also aware that, if your journey is anything like mine, there can be very real tension between how you feel *right now* versus what's *not yet reality.* What does success look like?

YOUR DEFINITION OF SUCCESS

I've wrestled with the idea of 'success' for a long time. While this book is for leaders, high performers and professionals of all stripes who want to break free from the stories holding them back, it's not overtly about 'success'.

As I've said, rewriting your story isn't a silver bullet. The Story Code won't solve all your problems – but it can make a massive difference.

In my life, I thought success was simple enough to define: strong relationships with my wife, kids and family. A growing business that can support our lifestyle in Sydney (one of the most expensive places to live on the planet). A sense of doing something meaningful. Naturally, none of these goals are bad at all. Yet when we use the Story Code to rewrite our stories, we raise the question of success in a different way. What should the ending look and feel like?

Like a movie director, it helps if you know where the story is going. I often look at the movie credits and marvel at the job title 'head of story'. Imagine if that person, who's one job is to understand and shape the movie's story from beginning to end, had no idea how it would wrap up. Obviously, none of us know how we will depart this wonderful planet of ours.

What I'm talking about, however, is how will you know you're successful on this journey from surviving to thriving? Well, I want to suggest a new perspective that could change the way you embark on this journey.

Success is keeping your lifestyle and dreams in sync.

Let's break it down.

When your new future story is coming into being, there are a few key intersecting elements we've discussed.

LIFESTYLE

Lifestyle is everything. Work meets home, play and service for the greater good. What's your ideal healthy lifestyle? Finding the right mythical work-life balance? For me it's:

- ✓ Maintaining physical wellbeing by caring about my food, sleep, exercise and relationships.
- ✓ Giving equal attention to matters of spiritual life, faith and serving. That looks different for each of us, but for me a recent aha in this space is the realisation that the disciplines I adopt aren't an end in themselves – they keep my heart and mind in check.
- ✓ Leaning into a meaningful, fulfilling career. Once again,

different for everyone. But a few tick boxes help me know whether I'm on the right track:

» Is my work meaningful?

» Can I best use and develop my skills?

» Is it sustainable? That is, does it give me energy and not leave me defeated?

» Is it psychologically safe? Life's too short, people!

DREAMS

Dreams is code for your ideal future *and* your ideal present, for instance, pursuing work that makes a difference and leaves plenty of room for family. What's your ideal daily reality?

IN SYNC

No, it's not a boy band. Keeping our lifestyles and dreams in sync is harder than it sounds, right? Life is unpredictable. People can be unkind. Children leave Lego on the floor, and the exquisite pain can make you question your life choices.

The quick illustration I want to share is something I learnt from my psychologist. Your relationship with your significant other moves between times when you feel really connected and close, and others when you could hardly be further apart. The decision we have to make is whether to keep deciding to come back together. It's easy enough to pull away – coming back together takes more effort. It's a choice.

All that being true, here are a few practical steps to help.

KEEP PERSPECTIVE WITH THE THREE S'S OF STORYTELLING

Firstly, where are you at in life? Beginning, middle or near the end? Remember the three S's of storytelling: setup, surprise, so what. To encode them briefly into this context:

- Your personal *setup* is where you're at right now. Self-doubt, burnout or some other mix of experiences.
- The *surprise*, I hope you've discovered, is how to use the Story Code to rewrite your narrative. The shadow story comes into the light. The opposite of your negative self-narrative becomes believably real.
- Then comes *so what?* You're not just changing your story. You're also changing your life.

ADAPTING THE BRAND JOURNEY

The Brand Journey model comprises six primary stages in the evolution of an organisation. It applies equally to our personal narrative, and for those of us in leadership, it's a super helpful way of thinking about our personal brand too.

Brand Journey Model

Here's how you can adapt the model and quickly get a sense of where you're at today. The 'setup' for your new story.

Each of us has an **origin story** that's a bit deeper than where we were born and lived as children. There's a moment or series of events that capture the essence of your identity and where you're from – perhaps it's the foundation of the rags-to-riches narrative.

To follow is the **vision story**. Whether early or later in life, this is the fun stuff. Dreaming of a career, a lifestyle, future family or perhaps a life in a completely different part of the world. It's the promise of big things coupled with a sense of adventure, or perhaps anxiety – *How can I bring this idea to life?*

Then we have one, or more likely *many*, **trial stories**. I've currently got two teenage boys, and, well, they're visceral reminders for me that growing up is anything but easy. My now adult daughter also endured her fair share of trials during teenage years. As adults, trials are a fact of life. But some are way bigger than others, and perhaps you're enduring one right now.

From there, we move to the **truth story** – a crisis or season during which things go from bad to worse. Will you go on? Or is there a temptation to give up and settle for a diminished existence? Again, no judgement here. The decisions we made and the connection between those moments and the present are key to reflecting on this story. Have you moved on, or perhaps you're still stuck? Are you counting the cost of what it will take to dive into a new adventure? Been there, done that!

Up next, the recovery. The phoenix, rebirth or recovery narrative as captured by your **growth story**. If you or someone in your circle has reinvented themselves or recovered from significant trauma, you'll know exactly what I'm talking about. Incredibly exciting and energising, the growth story dares us to appreciate the new season. Dig in and enjoy living!

Finally, the **destiny story**. My mind jumps to older Australians who've lived full and productive lives. They're inevitably generous with their time: volunteering, making time for the grandkids, serving in a community setting like church, sports clubs, community service organisations and so on. Likewise, adults of any age who've found themselves bringing their vision story to life are often inclined to give back: coaching, mentoring, investing in startups.

FROM SURVIVING TO THRIVING

The thing I love about the destiny stage of the journey is it can come at almost any point in our adult lives. We shift from a purely self-centred way of living to thinking less of ourselves and more of others. Sure, there's more to come – metaphorical mountains to climb. But someone who's thriving inevitably has energy to burn and capacity to help others. As Mahatma Gandhi famously said: "The best way to find yourself is to lose yourself in the service of others."

Inviting other people into the joy of your experience is part of the destiny story. Celebrating wins, goals achieved, birthdays reached and stupid selfies at conferences. It's easy to underplay these moments, but a destiny mindset is geared towards giving something of yourself.

Also related is the narrative of people who've experienced enormous change or trials. Perhaps they've faced a health crisis, job loss or crushing defeat. On the recovery journey, there's a fundamental desire to give back – a key feature of this destiny stage.

UP NEXT: HARD WORK

A friend of mine, Jonathan Browning, is a counsellor and pastor who has worked with some of the most broken people you can imagine. Working in a psych ward, his days were spent working with people experiencing schizophrenia, borderline personality disorder, bipolar, various addictions, anxiety and clinical depression. These people lived – or perhaps better expressed, 'existed' – at the extreme end of the wellbeing spectrum. Some were forcefully hospitalised and medicated. Others didn't have any clue who they were.

Then we've got his other life, now working with people in the community as a church pastor. The church, like the rest of society, is filled with people experiencing less extreme forms of suffering such as anxiety, depression and burnout. Yet even in this kinder, gentler environment, he said some people really struggle to show their real selves to others. He explained, "To engage and to belong and to fit is really, really hard work for them."

It's not lost on me that the work of rewriting our stories and taking small practical steps to reach out to others is enormously hard work. It's not that our environment, whether it's a church, workplace or community group, is overtly difficult or lacking empathy and compassion. Jonathan spoke about an 'intangible barrier' that prevents people from reaching out and making these small changes. What struck me about our conversation was a shared experience.

> I've also experienced a bit of shame and a real challenge wrestling with the idea that as a Christian, as a person who follows the Way, why is this anxiety still part of my reality? The Bible says let the peace of Christ rule in your hearts. Like, well, yeah, but I'm not feeling it. So we have this kind of existential crisis that we carry around with us.

That's an extraordinarily brave and honest thing to say. Jonathan is profoundly shining a light on the 'intangible barrier' that many of us discover in different settings – at work, home and social gatherings. Any tribe, culture or social group is united by the stories and unspoken expectations that define who's in and who's out.

As leaders in corporate environments, we've been talking about this existential crisis in terms of self-doubt, burnout and impostor phenomenon. "I'm the leader! I can't be suffering like this! What will they think of me!"

THE WAY FORWARD – BEING SEEN

Here's a profound insight Jonathan wrote about in his book, *Do You See Me?*, that had a significant impact on how I rewrote my story, and it might just light the way forward for you. Any person experiencing stress, trauma or trying to navigate their way through a tough time has one core, transformational desire: being seen. "The way of healing is vulnerability, which is both the gift and terror of being known. We cannot rush this and there are no short cuts."[1] The *gift* and *terror* of being known. Oh, my word. What a line.

It hit home for me recently when chatting with my colleague and friend of many years, Paula Cowan, who took over as managing director when I stepped down as CEO at ImpactInstitute to write this book and focus on professional speaking. A couple of months into my new life, she asked how it was all going. Without thinking too much, I blurted out: "It's exciting and terrifying!" So many opportunities, and so many unknowns. A gift to have the time to pursue my purpose and passion, and the terror of finding work and putting myself up on a stage where people literally judge your performance.

The parallel here is there are few moments in life, and particularly at work, when we let down our guard and really be ourselves. Yet when dealing with self-doubt and hidden inner narratives, that's exactly what we need. For Jonathan, his own experiences have fostered a capacity to have compassion for others experiencing self-doubt and the full spectrum of issues we've been discussing. So if we think about 'healing' in a broader sense – reclaiming confidence, becoming more resilient and building on the energy and joy that comes from rewriting your story – it's hard to move forward without daring to be vulnerable and be seen.

On the lighter side, a line from popular culture that comes to mind is, "I see you!" Urban Dictionary says it's a phrase used when someone understands where you're coming from, or they're impressed with you.[2]

It's an important distinction because we need to think about 'being seen' in more than a therapeutic context. Clearly, the workplace isn't an appropriate place for incredibly deep moments of vulnerability when our primary job is to get on with work. However, it's a reminder that the hard work of rewriting our stories is made a little easier when trusted friends and colleagues really can see you in a psychologically safe, appropriate way. Of course, it's nuanced, and each person's story will be different. But I'm yet to meet a team of workmates who don't know the ins and outs of one another's stories. Days and weeks on the job foster the kind of trust and mutual support that isn't just natural – it's *necessary*.

Gallup research shows that having a 'best friend' at work contributes to a thriving employee experience, improves communication, commitment to the job and other outcomes that make leaders happy – profitability, safety, inventory control and retention. Employees with best friends at work are better at engaging with customers and internal stakeholders, are more productive, experience fewer accidents, are better at innovating and sharing ideas, and have more fun.[3]

Now, I don't know what your relationships with best friends at work or in your personal life look like, but I'll tell you about my experience. I trust them. We share the highs and lows. They know how I'm *really* doing, and I'm not afraid to share. I know I'm seen, and I make a point of listening and talking to make sure they feel seen. And guess what? Research says that's all pretty normal. Strong social connections help lower the risk of suffering from health problems such as high blood pressure and unhealthy weight, and healthy social supports help us live longer.[4]

What's curious is that not all employers prioritise or acknowledge the value of these social bonds at work. The global polycrisis we've been talking about, our existential struggle with burnout, and the other issues discussed in this book all point to the simple fact that the workplace must become more socially and psychologically safe.

STORIES ARE SOCIAL

And yes, it's the stories and shared experiences that hold us together.

Studies show kids who grow up helping others and talking about their experiences have better mental health outcomes in life.[5] Adults who sign up to workplace giving programs are more engaged and satisfied at work – and, happily for employers, are more productive and less likely to leave.[6]

It follows that by rewriting your story and challenging yourself to face uncomfortable realities, you're ultimately crafting a new future self that helps yourself and others.

WHAT'S IT ALL GOOD FOR?

Let's cast forward and imagine you've started to realise my definition of success – keeping your lifestyle and dreams in sync. The enquiring mind could ask, *Then what?*

It could be the subject of another book, but existential questions about the meaning of life are inevitably part of this conversation for each of us. Beyond the obvious comedic answer – 42 ('to be') – the hunt for meaning is very much a mainstream conversation.[7] Meaning is one of the fundamental reasons we end up looking to rewrite our stories. A person's status quo is either meaningless, or not far off it. Just like my existential crisis on the streets of Sydney.

Are employers responsible for answering this question? Of course not. *You* don't even have to have an answer if you don't want to. But history shows that times of crisis for individuals, communities and societies inevitably inspire more people to grapple with existential questions.

A 2025 Global Flourishing Study surveyed 200,000 people

across 22 countries. Young adults in Western nations reported lower levels of life satisfaction compared to previous generations. They reported a perceived lack of meaning, greater financial insecurity and social isolation. At the same time, the traditional 'U-shaped' happiness curve is changing for the worse. Our happiness in youth, which dips in midlife and then returns in older age, is flattening out. Youth are increasingly unhappy, and in some countries, older people are flourishing less.[8]

No wonder books like Mark Manson's *Everything Is F*cked* are taking off. Mark ironically leans heavily into an existential, nihilistic and stoic world. Quoting Nietzsche, he talks about the elite and strong who were 'masters' of society (today's billionaire class), while the working masses were 'slaves' (today's wage slaves maybe?). The masters believed "might makes right" was a superior moral code, while the slaves celebrated their *weakness* as virtuous.[9] They're two value hierarchies that have strange resonance in today's geopolitical world. According to Nietzsche, this conflict between strong and weak is the root of all political and social conflict throughout history. Manson then makes the case that no amount of real or false hope can stop it.[10] So you're better off accepting the pain, suffering and messiness of life – like my 'shut up and suffer' friend. There's no hope for a better life, a better story. Therefore, we should act *without hope* because if nothing matters "there's no reason to *not* love ourselves and one another."[11]

DOES YOUR HEAD HURT YET?

I bring all this up because it taps into the depths of the existential crises many people in the working world and beyond are facing. Nowadays, younger generations – and people of all ages – seem to be rediscovering nihilistic beliefs driven by rising inequality, climate concerns, less religious Western societies and a general sense of powerlessness (Circles of Control and the Great Squeeze!).[12]

Everything must be meaningless, so why not just live for the moment?

I'm a big fan of UK indie rock singer-songwriter Sam Fender who sings about being a nihilist in the song 'Hypersonic Missiles'. For copyright reasons, I can't print the lyrics, but if you're curious, you can easily find the song and lyrics online. His take on finding meaning? Essentially, the world is doomed. He feels powerless. But he'll love anyway. Feels like a nod in Manson's and Nietzsche's general direction coupled with political advocacy. But you know what? As much as I love Fender's music and Manson's approach, it doesn't work for me.

I've already talked a bit about my faith and belief in the value of hope. I believe we can't simply ignore the deep human drive to live in service of something larger than ourselves. Comedian and philosopher Pete Holmes made me laugh with his attack on the 'nothingness' that pervades popular thought:

Some people think God created the universe. Some people think nothing created the universe. Which is the funniest guess?

And the 'nothing' people make fun of the 'God' people. They say, "God doesn't exist."

I'm like, "Okay, maybe." But you know what definitely doesn't exist? Nothing. That's the defining characteristic of nothing, is that it doesn't exist. So what are we talking about? Either you think it's God, something you can't see, touch, taste, photograph, and science can't prove, or you think it's nothing, something you can't see, touch, taste, photograph, and science can't prove.

But I think we can all agree if nothing, if your nothing sometimes spontaneously erupts into everything, that's a pretty goddamn magical f*cking nothing, you guys.

And ask the 'nothing' people, "What happens when you die?"

They'll tell you, "Nothing. You go into nothing."

I'm like, "You mean you merge back with your creator?"[13]

Holmes is expressing what Manson calls "the Uncomfortable Truth."[14]

UNLOCK A NEW EXISTENTIAL NARRATIVE WITH THE STORY CODE

The exciting part of this existential conversation and search for meaning is that it's an opportunity to again rewrite the narrative!

To live with joy and suffering, right and wrong, good and bad isn't a reason to give in and surrender. Susan Cain argues that embracing life's bitter and sweet moments leads to deeper creativity, connection and meaning.[15] We gain more, not less, by embracing both. Social psychologists such as Carol Anne Tavris and Elliot Aronson discuss this tension sparked by cognitive dissonance as an opportunity for personal growth and integrity.[16]

We can't simply let go of the stories, drop expectations and live with what *is*. Our memories remain, and our hearts and minds keep a record. The fundamental hope, the optimism I believe in, says there's always more to live and give. We don't have to pretend everything is fine or cede control over all aspects of our lives.

This conversation is about choosing to write a new storyline when you know deep down the old one no longer works. You're the master codebreaker and storyteller of your own life. You're in control of how you respond to the little moments, the big moments and the pursuit of your dreams. In fact, it's this foundational belief that lets you maintain a sense of control over your thoughts and emotions despite the circumstances.

Rewriting your story is proven to heal emotions, behaviours and improve physical wellbeing.[17] A healthier narrative can literally improve mental health and resilience. And yes, it produces a desire to work for the wellbeing of future generations and society at large – work that also delivers personal fulfillment and psychological wellbeing.

IT'S TIME TO THRIVE WITH YOUR NEW NARRATIVE

There's a good chance I'm preaching to the converted, but a risk we all face on this journey from self-doubt and survival mode to self-confidence and thriving is simply keeping it up. Your competition, if you like, isn't other people. It's apathy, comfort and losing the will to change.

So, a few parting suggestions and encouragement to stay strong.

Firstly, accountability matters. One of the simplest ways to keep moving forward is to think about a friend or partner. Who's the first person or group of people that comes to mind? Tell them about your story and see if they'd like to follow your journey as you rewrite your narrative.

Next, I've got a big challenge for you. What's the one thing in your future self, or future story, that scares you the most? Is it time to quit your job and start a new career? Maybe it's retraining, extra education or the time out needed to reset and refocus. This idea of facing your fears can also be thought of as *counting the cost*. Change can be costly in surprising ways. It's a lesson I've learnt more than once. As an entrepreneur, I've sold two houses for a combination of business and personal reasons. Massively stressful seasons, but an essential part of the journey.

UNLOCK YOUR IDEAL FUTURE

On that note, thank you for sharing this story with me.

As I said at the beginning, one of the reasons I'm so passionate about this topic stems from my discovery that re-writing our stories is one of the most important missing pieces in the puzzle of life. If this book goes even part way towards helping you rewrite your story to succeed and thrive on your own terms, job done. In fact, simply by reading this book, you've cracked the Story Code. You're now equipped to begin rewriting your narrative on your terms. You're ready to unlock your ideal future. The brain's already whirring, right?

In summary, the Story Code begins with the voice of your inner critic and ends with the voice of your inner coach being enacted every day.

- **Challenge** revealed the lies of the critic and your limiting beliefs. We named the dragon.
- **Overwrite** gave you a new archetype and a new lens to reframe meaning.

- **Decide** helped you commit to a future story.
- **Encode** ensures that story lasts with healthy habits.

The Story Code is more than a framework – it's a practice. And as research shows, practice leads to neural rewiring, stronger self-compassion and the freedom to lead with clarity, confidence and courage.

To borrow Maya Angelou's words, there's no greater agony than an untold story inside you.[18] The real question is – will you confront the dragon and rewrite your story? The next move is yours.

Onwards.

ACKNOWLEDGEMENTS

My Creator. The greatest storyteller of them all.
Heather, my wife and best friend, thank you for creating the space to help me write this book. Your patience, commitment to our journey and sharp insights have taken this work to another level.

Emily, Daniel, Toby and Ethan. Being your dad is the *best ever*. Thanks for your love, support and understanding – particularly when Dad's still in his office writing *the book* and you'd rather I was doing something with you.

Susan Dean, Natalie Deane, Matt Moore, Meng Koach and the team at Dean Publishing. We got there! You guys are a class act, and I'm grateful for your professionalism, care and commitment to this project.

To the ten leaders who shared their stories with me: Belinda Elworthy, Daniel Davis, David Newman, Jonathan Browning,

Mark Yettica-Paulson, Nicola Nel, Dr Renu Burr, Sasha Titchkosky, Steve Vamos, and Tim Washer. Your generosity and insights brought this story to life. Thank you.

Phil Henry and Kath Henry. I love you guys so much. Thanks for sharing your cottage on a glorious hill in Gloucester – the most perfect retreat an author could dream about.

My friends in Professional Speakers Australia, with a special shout-out to Lindsay Adams, Gary Edwards and Chris Wildeboer. Speaking is indeed a strange business, yet you make it strangely normal and fun (partly because you appreciate my Monty Python references).

Paula Cowan, Royden Howie, Kate Zadel and all my colleagues at ImpactInstitute. Your support and friendship has made this book possible. Onwards!

To my clients and work friends here in Australia and around the world. Doing work you love is one of life's great privileges. Thanks for the opportunity to be part of your stories and create new stories together that make a difference.

Finally to you, dear reader, thanks for picking up a copy and giving me your time and attention – in a digital world, it's not something I take for granted! This book is ultimately not about me; it's about you and your journey. So here's to slaying dragons and bringing your new story to life – the world needs it now more than ever.

ABOUT THE AUTHOR

Mark Jones is an author, journalist, executive coach and mindset strategist who transforms high-performance leaders and teams.

A Certified Speaking Professional (CSP) and entrepreneur, he helps professionals rewrite the stories they tell themselves to build resilience and increase influence.

Mark's work draws on a rare combination of storytelling mastery, leadership and business expertise. His keynotes and workshops are high-energy, insightful and entertaining – blending storytelling, mindset transformation and practical leadership tools refined over 30 years working in global media, marketing and business.

He has delivered entertaining and heartfelt messages to thousands of people across five continents for 17 years.

The Story Code is his second book. *Beliefonomics: Realise the True Value of Your Brand Story* (2020) was launched the week before COVID-19 changed the world (hot tip, don't launch books during a pandemic!).

Away from work, Mark is a husband and father of four children and one much-loved dog. Family life is an unpredictable, glorious, ever-unfolding story that probably deserves its own book, or at least a comedy sketch.

Read more about his work at markjones.au

ENDNOTES

Introduction

1   Bryson B (2000) *Down Under: Travels in a Sunburned Country,* Transworld Digital.

2   World Population Review (2025) 'Dhaka Population 2025', accessed 8 August 2025, https://worldpopulationreview.com/cities/bangladesh/dhaka; World Population Review (2025) 'Shanghai Population 2025', accessed 8 August 2025, https://worldpopulationreview.com/cities/china/shanghai.

Chapter 1

1   Working Genius (2022) 'The 6 Types of Working Genius: Genius Pairings Overview', *The Table Group,* accessed 8 August 2025, files.tablegroup.com/wp-content/uploads/2022/10/11030500/Working-Genius-Pairings-Overview.pdftablegroup.com.

2   Steptoe A, Dockray S, and Wardle J (2009) 'Positive Affect and Psychobiological Processes Relevant to Health', *Journal of Personality*, 77(6):1747–76, doi.org/10.1111/j.1467-6494.2009.00599.x.

3   Williams D and Sternthal M (2007) 'Spirituality, Religion and Health: Evidence and Research Directions', *Medical Journal of Australia*, 186, doi.org/10.5694/j.1326-5377.2007.tb01040.x.

4   Ramamurthy C, Zuo P, Armstrong G, and Andriessen K (2024) 'The Impact of Storytelling on Building Resilience in Children: A Systematic Review', *Journal of Psychiatric and Mental Health Nursing*, 31(4):525–542, doi.org/10.1111/jpm.13008.

5   Strawson G (10 January 2004) 'Tales of the Unexpected', *The Guardian,* accessed 8 August 2025, https://www.theguardian.com/books/2004/jan/10/society.philosophy.

6   McAdams, DP (1993) *The Stories We Live By: Personal Myths and the Making of the Self,* Guilford Press.

7   McAdams DP and McClean KC (2013) 'Narrative Identity', *Association for Psychological Science,* 22(3), doi.org/10.1177/0963721413475622.

8   BCG (11 June 2024) 'Half of Workers Around the World Are Struggling with Burnout', accessed 29 September 2025, https://www.bcg.com/press/11june2024-half-of-workers-around-the-world-struggling-with-burnout.

9   Fair Work Ombudsman (n.d.) 'Right to Disconnect', *Australian Government,*

accessed 29 September 2025, https://www.fairwork.gov.au/employment-conditions/hours-of-work-breaks-and-rosters/right-to-disconnect.

10   SafeWork NSW (n.d.) 'Code of Practice: Managing Psychosocial Hazards at Work', *NSW Government*, accessed 29 September 2025, https://www.safework.nsw.gov.au/resource-library/list-of-all-codes-of-practice/codes-of-practice/managing-psychosocial-hazards-at-work.

11   AIHS (2025) 'WHS Prosecutions Rise with $164 Million in Penalties Since 2020', accessed 29 September 2025, https://www.aihs.org.au/Web/Web/Advocacy-Media/All-News/2025/07-July/WHS%20prosecutions%20climb%20as%20Safe%20Work%20Australia%20tracks%20%24164%20million%20in%20penalties.aspx.

12   EML (2025) 'Inside the Minds of Australia's Workplaces: Evidence, Insight, and Collective Action for Better Mental Health Outcomes', accessed 29 September 2025, https://www.eml.com.au/wp-content/uploads/2025/06/EML_Mental-Health-White-Paper_Inside-the-Minds-of-Australias-Workplaces_WEB.pdf.

13   WHO (2 September 2024) 'Mental Health at Work', accessed 29 September 2025, https://www.who.int/news-room/fact-sheets/detail/mental-health-at-work.

14   Goldsmith M (2008) *What Got You Here Won't Get You There: How Successful People Become Even More Successful,* Profile Business.

15   Benefolk (23 October 2023) 'Leaders Call for Immediate Action to Tackle and Prevent Burnout in Social Sector', accessed 9 August 2025, https://benefolk.org/about/news?view=article&id=3222:leaders-call-for-immediate-action-to-tackle-and-prevent-burnout-in-social-sector.

16   Benefolk (2020) 'Reset 2020: National Impact+Need Research Study Phase 2 - September 2020 Survey Interval', accessed 9 August 2025, https://bene-folk.org/component/edocman/reset-2020-research-study-report-phase-2/viewdocument/39?Itemid=0.

17   Denborough D (2014) *Retelling the Stories of Our Lives: Everyday Narrative Therapy to Draw Inspiration and Transform Experience,* W. W. Norton and Company:21.

18   Denborough D (2014) *Retelling the Stories of Our Lives: Everyday Narrative Therapy to Draw Inspiration and Transform Experience,* W. W. Norton and Company.

19   Denborough D (2014) *Retelling the Stories of Our Lives: Everyday Narrative Therapy to Draw Inspiration and Transform Experience,* W. W. Norton and Company.

20   Denborough D (2014) *Retelling the Stories of Our Lives: Everyday Narrative Therapy to Draw Inspiration and Transform Experience,* W. W. Norton and Company:159.

21   Loehr J (2008) *The Power of Story: Change Your Story, Change Your Destiny in Business and in Life,* Free Press.

22   Manson M (2016) *The Subtle Art of Not Giving a F*ck: A Counterintuitive Approach to Living a Good Life,* Macmillan Australia.

23 And Metallica for All (30 November) 'Lars Ulrich and Dave Mustaine Interview Complete Scenes 2001 The Most Memorable Scenes - English Sub' [video], YouTube, accessed 29 September 2025, https://www.youtube.com/watch?v=KecXxv-GuTY.

Chapter 2

1   Tuohy W (12 January 2024) 'Kylie Moore-Gilbert: From "Childless Divorcee with a Criminal Record" to Motherhood and a Mission', *Sydney Morning Herald,* accessed 8 August 2025, https://www.smh.com.au/national/kylie-moore-gilbert-from-childless-divorcee-with-a-criminal-record-to-motherhood-and-a-mission-20231219-p5eshd.html.

2   Jackson I (28 May 2025) 'Exclusive: Seven in 10 Women Experience Imposter Syndrome at Work, Research Finds', *People Management,* accessed 8 August 2025, https://www.peoplemanagement.co.uk/article/1919598/exclusive-seven-10-women-experience-imposter-syndrome-work-research-finds.

3   Headspace (2024) 'Workforce State of Mind: Sixth Annual Workplace Mental Health Trends Report', accessed 8 August 2025, https://get.headspace.com/2024-workforce-state-of-mind.

4   Karmali M (28 January 2025) 'Over Half of American Employees Have Used AI to Take Workplace Training, According to New Data', *Moodle,* accessed 8 August 2025, https://moodle.com/us/news/ai-for-workplace-training-in-america/.

5   Martinez MF, O'Shea KJ, Kern MC, White C, Dibbs AM, and Lee BY (2025) 'The Health and Economic Burden of Employee Burnout to U.S. Employers', *American Journal of Preventative Medicine,* 68(4):645–655, https://www.ajpmonline.org/article/S0749-3797(25)00023-6/.

6   Herbst CM (2011) '"Paradoxical" Decline? Another Look at the Relative Reduction in Female Happiness', *Journal of Economic Psychology,* 32(5):773–788, doi.org/10.1016/j.joep.2011.07.001.

7   Piao X, Xie J, and Managi S (2024) 'Continuous Worsening of Population Emotional Stress Globally: Universality and Variations', *BMC Public Health,* 24, doi.org/10.1186/s12889-024-20961-4.

8   Klerman, GL and Weissman MM (1989) 'Increasing Rates of Depression', *JAMA,* 261(15):2229–2235, https://pubmed.ncbi.nlm.nih.gov/2648043/; Twenge JM (2015) 'Time Period and Birth Cohort Differences in Depressive Symptoms in the U.S., 1982–2013', *Social Indicators Research,* 121(2):437–454, doi.org/10.1007/s11205-014-0647-1.

9   Microsoft (22 September 2022) 'Hybrid Work Is Just Work. Are We Doing It Wrong?' accessed 8 August 2025, https://www.microsoft.com/en-us/worklab/work-trend-index/hybrid-work-is-just-work.

10   Small Business Connection (26 February 2025) 'Workplace Burnout
     Surges: 2 in 5 Aussie Employees Already Exhausted in 2025', https://
     smallbusinessconnections.com.au/workplace-burnout-surges-2-in-5-auss-
     ie-employees-already-exhausted-in-2025; Glover F (18 March 2025)
     'Australian Workers Face Rising Levels of Burnout in the Workplace', accessed
     8 August 2025, https://www.staffingindustry.com/news/global-daily-news/
     australian-workers-face-rising-levels-of-burnout-in-the-workplace.

11   Gallup (2025) 'State of the Global Workplace: Understanding Employees,
     Informing Leaders', accessed 8 August 2025, https://www.gallup.com/work-
     place/349484/state-of-the-global-workplace.aspx.

12   Infinite Potential (2025) 'The State of Workplace Burnout 2025: Strategies for
     a Sustainable Workforce', *AIOH,* accessed 8 August 2025. https://aihs.org.au/
     common/Uploaded%20files/Learning-and-Events/Webinar%20Presentation/2025/
     The%20State%20of%20Workplace%20Burnout%20%20Webinar%20Slides.pdf

13   Sunriseon7 (17 March 2025) Instagram post, accessed 8 August 2025, https://www.
     instagram.com/reel/DHRjkGssJpQ/.

14   AIHW (2025) 'Monthly Suicide Registers', accessed 8 August 2025, https://
     www.aihw.gov.au/suicide-self-harm-monitoring/geography/states-territories/
     monthly-suicide-registers.

15   AIHW (20 May 2025) 'Prevalence and Impact of Mental Illness', ac-
     cessed 8 August 2025, https://www.aihw.gov.au/mental-health/overview/
     prevalence-and-impact-of-mental-illness.

16   Australian Psychological Society (4 June 2025) 'More Men Will Slip Through
     the Cracks Unless Rapid Action Is Taken, Says Peak Psychology Body', ac-
     cessed 8 August 2025, https://psychology.org.au/about-us/news-and-media/
     media-releases/2025/more-men-will-slip-through-the-cracks-unless-rapid.

17   WHO (8 June 2022) 'Mental Disorders', accessed 8 August 2025, https://www.
     who.int/news-room/fact-sheets/detail/mental-disorders.

18   Grantham-Philips W (6 February 2025) 'Workday Lays
     Off 1,750 Employees, or About 8.5% of Its Workforce',
     AP, accessed 12 August 2025, https://apnews.com/article/
     workday-layoffs-job-cuts-ai-investments-437581ad79d6e1cef2de7b300015dfbb.

19   Kauflin J (4 May 2025) 'It's Time to Get Concerned as More Companies Replace
     Workers With AI', *Forbes,* accessed 12 August 2025, https://www.forbes.com/sites/
     jackkelly/2025/05/04/its-time-to-get-concerned-klarna-ups-duolingo-cisco-and-ma-
     ny-other-companies-are-replacing-workers-with-ai/.

20   Corrall C, Stringer A, and Park K (22 September2025) 'A Comprehensive List of
     2025 Tech Layoffs', *TechCrunch,* accessed 30 September 2025, https://techcrunch.
     com/2025/08/29/tech-layoffs-2025-list/.

21 Foster T (2–3 July 2025) 'Doughnut Economics Session at Social Impact Summit', *ImpactInstitute*.

22 Didion J (1979) *The White Album,* Simon & Schuster.

23 Covey S (1989) *The 7 Habits of Highly Effective People: 30th Anniversary Edition,* Free Press.

24 Minchin T (5 December 2024) 'Tim Minchin on His Viral Speech, Quitting Social Media and Being Kind', *Channel 4 News,* YouTube, accessed 12 August 2025, https://youtu.be/H9wRL8QLmO4.

25 McCurry J (2023) 'Isolation nation: Japan Tries to Draw Its Citizens Out of Post-Covid Seclusion', *The Guardian,* accessed 13 August 2025, https://www.theguardian.com/world/2023/may/12/isolation-nation-one-in-50-japanese-living-in-seclusion-after-covid.

26 HealthyFitness1374 (8 January 2025) 'What Do About Students Are Apathetic and Lazy About Life.', *Reddit,* accessed 30 September 2025, https://www.reddit.com/r/Teachers/comments/1hw12pl/what_do_about_students_are_apathetic_and_lazy/.

27 Solomon A (30 September 2024) 'Has Social Media Fuelled a Teen-Suicide Crisis?', *The New Yorker,* accessed 13 August 2025, https://www.newyorker.com/magazine/2024/10/07/social-media-mental-health-suicide-crisis-teens.

28 Melbourne Institute (n.d.) 'HILDA Survey', *University of Melbourne,* accessed 13 August 2025, https://melbourneinstitute.unimelb.edu.au/hilda; University of Melbourne (12 February 2024) 'HILDA Data Shows Psychological Distress Rising, Loneliness Highest Amongst Young People', accessed 13 August 2025, https://www.unimelb.edu.au/newsroom/news/2024/february/hilda-data-shows-psychological-distress-rising,-loneliness-highest-amongst-young-people.

29 The Associated Press (24 October 2012) 'Number of Active Users at Facebook Over the Years', *Yahoo! News,* accessed 13 August 2025, https://www.yahoo.com/news/finance/news/trump-bringing-much-revenue-tariffs-182932609.html.

30 LinkedIn Corporate Communications (11 April 2007) 'LinkedIn Professional Network Reaches 10 Million Users', *LinkedIn,* accessed 13 August 2025, https://news.linkedin.com/2007/04/linkedin-professional-network-reaches-10-million-users.

31 Johnson B and Glendinning L (10 January 2007) 'Apple Proclaims Its Revolution: A Camera, an iPod … Oh, and a Phone', *The Guardian,* accessed 13 August 2025, https://www.theguardian.com/technology/2007/jan/10/news.business.

32 University of Melbourne (12 February 2024) 'HILDA Data Shows Psychological Distress Rising, Loneliness Highest Amongst Young People', accessed 13 August 2025, https://www.unimelb.edu.au/newsroom/news/2024/february/hilda-data-shows-psychological-distress-rising,-loneliness-highest-amongst-young-people.

33 Marinos S (12 February 2024) 'The "Perfect Storm" Causing Australians Psychological Distress', *University of Melbourne*, accessed 13 August 2025, https://pursuit.unimelb.edu.au/articles/the-perfect-storm-causing-australians-psychological-distress.

34 Mackay H (2021) *The Kindness Revolution: How We Can Restore Hope, Rebuild Trust and Inspire Optimism*, Allen & Unwin:107–108.

35 Fleuren BPI, Nübold A, Uitdewilligen S, Verduyn P, and Hülsheger UR (2023) 'Troubles on Troubled Minds: An Intensive Longitudinal Diary Study on the Role of Burnout in the Resilience Process Following Acute Stressor Exposure', *European Journal of Work and Organizational Psychology*, 32(3):373–388, doi.org/10.1080/13 59432X.2022.2161369.

36 Dulaney M and Uebergang K (4 March 2025) 'The Ethical Dilemmas Surrounding Inherited Wealth', *ABC News*, accessed 13 August 2025, https://www.abc.net.au/news/2025-03-04/great-wealth-transfer-ethics-of-inheritance/104990138.

37 Sanders B (2 September 2022) 'The US Has a Ruling Class – and Americans Must Stand Up to It', *The Guardian*, accessed 13 August 2025, https://www.theguardian.com/commentisfree/2022/sep/02/the-us-has-a-ruling-class-and-americans-must-stand-up-to-it.

38 DeSilver D (7 August 2018) 'For Most U.S. Workers, Real Wages Have Barely Budged in Decades', *Pew Research Center*, accessed 13 August 2025, https://www.pewresearch.org/short-reads/2018/08/07/for-most-us-workers-real-wages-have-barely-budged-for-decades/.

39 Davidson P, Bradbury B, and Wong M (2024) 'Inequality in Australia 2024: Who Is Affected and How', *ACOSS*, accessed 13 August 2025, doi.org/10.5281/zenodo.15208516.

40 ACOSS (2024) 'Inequality in Australia', accessed 13 August 2025, https://povertyandinequality.acoss.org.au/inequality/.

41 Trainer T (2021) 'Third World Development: The Simpler Way Critique of Conventional Theory and Practice', *Real-World Economics Review*, 95, https://www.paecon.net/PAEReview/issue95/Trainer95.pdf.

42 Hickel J (2017) 'Is Global Inequality Getting Better or Worse? A Critique of the World Bank's Convergence Narrative', *Third World Quarterly*, 38(10):2208–2222, doi.org/10.1080/01436597.2017.1333414.

43 Chang HJ (2010) *23 Things They Don't Tell You About Capitalism*, Penguin.

44 ABC News (28 November 2010) '"This Week" Transcript: The Giving Pledge', accessed 13 August 2025, https://abcnews.go.com/ThisWeek/week-transcript-giving-pledge/story?id=12258827.

45 Australian Unity (2024) 'Australian Unity Wellbeing Index: Survey 41',

accessed 13 August 2025, https://www.australianunity.com.au/wellbeing/the-australian-unity-wellbeing-index.

46 Centre for Policy Development (22 March 2025) '2025 Purpose of Government Pulse', accessed 13 August 2025, https://cpd.org.au/work/2025-purpose-of-government-pulse/.

47 Jones M (October 2023) 'How the Marketing Academy Is Boosting Marketers to the Boardroom' [podcast], *The CMO Show,* Spotify, accessed 13 August 2025, https://open.spotify.com/episode/22NlOygkc5oFYgTUlKRAkO?si=AhbF8ovdSMmVzPtHR1OEAg.

Chapter 3

1 Shojaee P, Mirzadeh I, Alizadeh K, Horton M, Bengio S, and Farajtabar M (2025) 'The Illusion of Thinking: Understanding the Strengths and Limitations of Reasoning Models via the Lens of Problem Complexity', *Apple,* accessed 25 August 2025, https://ml-site.cdn-apple.com/papers/the-illusion-of-thinking.pdf.

2 Jennings LE and McLean KC (2013) 'Storying Away Self-Doubt: Can Narratives Dispel Threats to the Self?', *Journal of Research in Personality,* 47(4):317–329, doi.org/10.1016/j.jrp.2013.02.006.

3 Beachley L (18 July 2015) 'The Power of Self-Belief | Layne Beachley | TEDxStHildasSchool' [video], *TEDx Talks,* YouTube, accessed 26 August 2025, https://www.youtube.com/watch?v=CKVSjIIt8t0.

4 Dweck C (2013) *Mindset: How You Can Fulfil Your Potential: Changing the Way You think To Fulfil Your Potential,* Constable & Robinson.

5 Waititi T (2009) 'Evicted' [television program], *Flight of the Conchords* (season 2, episode 10), Dakota Pictures.

Chapter 4

1 Philippians 4:4-8.

2 Huffington A (2014) *Thrive: The Third Metric to Redefining Success and Creating a Happier Life,* Virgin Digital.

3 The Weekly (3 May 2024) 'Savage Review of Play School | The Weekly | ABC TV + iview' [video], *ABC iview,* YouTube, accessed 14 August 2025, https://youtu.be/4qMm5mH8AnQ.

4 Stone H and Stone S (1994) 'The Inner Critic', *Voice Dialogue International,* accessed 14 August 2025, https://voicedialogueinternational.com/articles/The_Inner_Critic.htm.

5 McLeod S (13 March 2025) 'Id, Ego, and Superego', *Simply Psychology,* accessed 14

August 2025, https://www.simlypsychology.org/psyche.html.

6   McLeod S (18 March 2025) 'Vygotsky's Theory of Cognitive Development', *Simply Psychology*, accessed 14 August 2025, https://www.simlypsychology.org/vygotsky.html.

7   Bateman J, Hayes S, and Arnett W (hosts) (9 December 2024) 'Daniel Craig' [podcast], *SmartLess*, accessed 1 October 2025.

8   Hendrikson E (2018) *How to Be Yourself: Quiet Your Inner Critic and Rise Above Social Anxiety*, St Martin's Press.

9   White M (2024) *Maps of Narrative Practice,* W. W. Norton & Company.

10   Vitoria DA (2021) 'Experiential Supervision: Healing Imposter Phenomenon from the Inside Out', *The Clinical Supervisor,* 40(2):200–217, doi.org/10.1080/0732522 3.2020.1830215.

11   EOS (n.d.) 'About EOS Worldwide', accessed 15 August 2025, https://www.eosworldwide.com/eos-history-team.

12   Reimbold B (23 November 2020) 'IDS™', *EOS,* accessed 15 August 2025, https://www.eosworldwide.com/implementer-posts/ids-make-your-meetings-matter-again.

13   Australian Institute of Family Studies (September 2020) 'Depression, Suicidality and Loneliness: Mental Health and Australian Men', *Australian Government,* accessed 15 August 2025, https://aifs.gov.au/tentomen/media/depression-suicidality-and-loneliness-mental-health-and-australian-men.

14   Australian Bureau of Statistics (10 October 2024) 'Causes of Death, Australia', accessed 15 August 2025, https://www.abs.gov.au/statistics/health/causes-death/causes-death-australia/latest-release.

15   Birrell L, Prior K, Vescovi J, Sunderland M, Slade T, and Chapman C (2025) 'Treatment Rates and Delays for Mental and Substance Use Disorders: Results from the Australian National Survey of Mental Health and Wellbeing', *Epidemiology and Psychiatric Sciences,* 34, doi.org/10.1017/S2045796025000034.

16   Epston D and White M (2023) *Narrative Means to Therapeutic Ends,* W. W. Norton & Company.

Chapter 5

1   Manson M (n.d.) 'How to Overcome Your Limiting Beliefs', accessed 15 August 2025, https://markmanson.net/limiting-beliefs.

2   Jones M (2020) *Beliefonomics: Realise the True Value of Your Brand Story,* Beliefonomics Pty Ltd.

3   Rich Roll (15 February 2023) 'Stories Make Life Livable | Robert McKee'

[video], YouTube, accessed 1 October 2025, https://www.youtube.com/
watch?v=I5v6KwPxyFs.

4   Raypole C (16 June 2020) 'It's Totally Normal (and Healthy) to Talk to Yourself',
Healthline, accessed 21 August 2025, https://www.healthline.com/health/
why-do-i-talk-to-myself.

5   Dweck C (2017) *Mindset: Changing the Way You Think to Fulfil Your
Potential,* Robinson.

6   Connors MH and Halligan PW (2015) A Cognitive Account of Belief: A Tentative
Road Map', *Frontiers in Psychology,* 5, doi.org/10.3389/fpsyg.2014.01588.

Chapter 6

1   Freedman L (7 January 2025) 'How Brooke Shields Overrides Her Inner Critic
(Yes, She Has One!)', *Real Simple,* accessed 22 August 2025, https://www.real-
simple.com/how-brooke-shields-overrides-her-inner-critic-8762866.

2   Freedman L (7 January 2025) 'How Brooke Shields Overrides Her Inner Critic
(Yes, She Has One!)', *Real Simple,* accessed 22 August 2025, https://www.real-
simple.com/how-brooke-shields-overrides-her-inner-critic-8762866.

3   Entwistle J (director) (2025) *Karate Kid: Legends* [motion picture],
Columbia Pictures.

4   Avildsen JG (director) (1984) *Karate Kid* [motion picture], Delphi II Productions.

5   Jung CG (1968) *The Archetypes and the Collective Unconscious,* 2nd edn, Princeton
University Press.

6   Campbell J (2008) *The Hero with a Thousand Faces,* New World Library.

7   Epston D and White M (2023) *Narrative Means to Therapeutic Ends,* W. W.
Norton & Company.

8   Vogler C (2007) *The Writer's Journey: Mythic Structure for Writers,* Michael Wiese
Productions.

9   Rovetta FF (2023) 'The Dual Role of Inner Speech in Narrative Self-Understanding
and Narrative Self-Enactment', *Review of Philosophy and Psychology,* 15: 975–995,
doi.org/10.1007/s13164-023-00690-0.

Chapter 7

1   Netflix (2021) 'Brainwashing' [television program], *The Mind, Explained* (season 2,
episode 5), Netflix.

Chapter 8

1   Jennings LE and McLean KC (2013) 'Storying Away Self-Doubt: Can Narratives Dispel Threats to the Self?', *Journal of Research in Personality*, 47(4):317–329, doi. org/10.1016/j.jrp.2013.02.006.

2   Sloan DM and Marx BP (2004) 'A Closer Examination of the Structured Written Disclosure Procedure', *Journal of Consulting and Clinical Psychology*, 72(2):165–175, doi.org/10.1037/0022-006X.72.2.165; Baikie KA and Wilhelm K (2005) 'Emotional and Physical Health Benefits of Expressive Writing', *Advances in Psychiatric Treatment*, 11:338–346, doi.org/10.1192/apt.11.5.338.

3   Maven Team (2024) 'Beyond the Basics: How HR Leaders Can Support Mental Health Along the Family Journey', *Maven Clinic,* accessed 26 August 2025, https:// www.mavenclinic.com/post/hr-mental-health.

4   Jennings LE and McLean KC (2013) 'Storying Away Self-Doubt: Can Narratives Dispel Threats to the Self?', *Journal of Research in Personality*, 47(4):317–329, doi. org/10.1016/j.jrp.2013.02.006.

5   Duan S, Chu W, and Liu H (2023) 'Seeking Resilience, Sustaining Development: A Self-Narrative Study of Early Career English Teacher Resilience', *Sustainability*, 15(16):12386, doi.org/10.3390/su151612386.

Chapter 9

1   Pennebaker JW (1997) 'Writing About Emotional Experiences as a Therapeutic Process', *Psychological Science*, 8(3):162–166, doi.org/10.1111/j.1467-9280.1997. tb00403.x; Ruini C and Mortara CC (2022) 'Writing Technique Across Psychotherapies-From Traditional Expressive Writing to New Positive Psychology Interventions: A Narrative Review', *Journal of Contemporary Psychotherapy*, 52(1):23–34, doi.org/10.1007/s10879-021-09520-9.

2   Otitigbe J (30 November 2016) 'Remembering the Sounds of the World's Most Iconic Deep Listening Pioneer: Pauline Oliveros', *RPI,* accessed 29 August 2025, https://news.rpi.edu/content/2016/11/30/ remembering-deep-listener-pioneer-pauline-oliveros.

3   Trimboli O (n.d.) 'Podcast Episode 052: The Five Levels of Listening – The Big Picture' [podcast], *Deep Listening,* accessed 29 August 2025, https://www.oscartrim-boli.com/podcast/052/.

4   Clear J (2018) *Atomic Habits: An Easy and Proven Way to Build Good Habits and Break Bad Ones,* Cornerstone Digital.

5   Fazio LK (2020) 'Repetition Increases Perceived Truth Even for Known Falsehoods', *Collabra: Psychology*, 6(1):38, doi.org/10.1525/collabra.347; Jeremiah F, Butson

R, and Oke A (2025) 'New Perspectives on Repetitive Behaviour', *Psychological Research*, 89(2):61, doi.org/10.1007/s00426-025-02092-6; Shehata A (2025) 'News Coverage and the Social Dimension of Belief Reinforcement: A Longitudinal Mixed-Methods Approach', *Human Communication Research*, 5(2)112–125, doi.org/10.1093/hcr/hqae020.

6   UEN (n.d.) 'Introduction – a Practicum in Behavioral Economics', accessed 29 August 2025, https://uen.pressbooks.pub/behavioraleconomics/front-matter/introduction/.

Chapter 10

1   Ghavibazou E, Hosseinian S, Ghamari kivi H, and Ebrahim NA (2022) 'Narrative Therapy, Applications, and Outcomes: A Systematic Review', *Preventive Counseling*, 2(4): doi.org/10.2139/ssrn.4119920.

Chapter 11

1   Browning J (n.d.) *Do You See Me?*.

2   The Salty Sailor (2 July 2016) 'I See You', *Urban Dictionary*, accessed 2 September 2025, https://www.urbandictionary.com/define.php?term=I+see+you.

3   Patel A and Plowman S (16 August 2022) 'The Increasing Importance of a Best Friend at Work', *Gallup,* accessed 2 September 2025, https://www.gallup.com/workplace/397058/increasing-importance-best-friend-work.aspx.

4   Holt-Lunstad J (2021) 'Loneliness and Social Isolation as Risk Factors: The Power of Social Connection in Prevention', *American Journal of Lifestyle Medicine*, 15(5):567–573, doi.org/10.1177/15598276211009454; CDC (15 May 2024) 'Social Connection', accessed 2 September 2025, https://www.cdc.gov/social-connectedness/about/.

5   Rowland B and Evans-Whipp T (May 2023) 'Prosocial Behaviours and the Positive Impact on Mental Health', *Australian Institute of Family Studies,* accessed 2 September 2025, https://aifs.gov.au/growing-australia/research/research-snapshots/prosocial-behaviours-and-positive-impact-mental.

6   Workplace Giving Australia (2024) 'Giving Research & Insights 2024', accessed 2 September 2025, https://26897743.fs1.hubspotusercontent-eu1.net/hubfs/26897743/Workplace%20Giving%20Australia%20Research%202024%20Analysis.pdf.

7   JosehfMurchison (14 February 2018) 'The True Meaning of 42 in The Hitchhikers Guide to the Galaxy' [online forum post], *Reddit,* https://www.reddit.com/r/FanTheories/comments/7xbcdx/the_true_meaning_of_42_in_the_hitchhikers_guide/.

8   VanderWeele TJ, Johnson BR, Bialowolski PT et al. (2025) 'The Global Flourishing Study: Study Profile and Initial Results on Flourishing', *Nature Mental Health,* 3:636–653 doi.org/10.1038/s44220-025-00423-5.

9   Manson M (2019) *Everything Is F*cked: A Book About Hope,* Harper.

10   Manson M (2019) *Everything Is F*cked: A Book About Hope,* Harper.

11   Manson M (2019) *Everything Is F*cked: A Book About Hope,* Harper.

12   Bradley S (25 April 2022) 'Why More Young People Are Turning to Nihilism', *Huck Magazine,* accessed 2 September 2025, https://www.huckmag.com/article/why-more-young-people-are-turning-to-nihilism.

13   Holmes P (22 February 2024) 'Pete Holmes: I Am Not for Everyone (2023) | Transcript', *Scraps from the Loft,* accessed 2 September 2025, https://scraps-fromtheloft.com/comedy/pete-holmes-i-am-not-for-everyone-transcript/.

14   Manson M (2019) *Everything Is F*cked: A Book About Hope,* Harper.

15   Cain S (2023) *Bittersweet: How Sorrow and Longing Make Us Whole,* Crown Publishing Group.

16   Wikipedia (7 February 2025) 'Carol Tavris', accessed 3 October 2025, https://en.wikipedia.org/wiki/Carol_Tavris.

17   Khodayarifard M and Sohrabpour G (2018) 'Effectiveness of Narrative Therapy in Groups on Psychological Well-Being and Distress of Iranian Women with Addicted Husbands', *Addiction and Health,* 10(1):1–10, doi.org/10.22122/ahj.v10i1.550.

18   Angelou M (1969) *I Know Why the Caged Bird Sings,* Random House: 192.

www.ingramcontent.com/pod-product-compliance
Lightning Source LLC
Chambersburg PA
CBHW030458210326
41597CB00013B/719